CRYSTAL PERSONALITIES
A Quick Reference
To Special Forms of Crystal

By Patricia Troyer

Illustrations by Eric Lovstad

1995

STONE PEOPLE PUBLISHING COMPANY
Peoria, Arizona

CRYSTAL PERSONALITIES:
A Quick Reference To
Special Forms of Crystal

By Patricia Troyer

Published by:

Stone People Publishing Company
7445 W. Cactus Rd., #211, Box 195
Peoria, AZ 85381

This book is a reference book based upon research by the author and those listed in the Bibliography.

Requests for permission to reprint, reproduce, etc. to:

Patricia Troyer
7118 W. Paradise Dr.
Peoria, AZ 85345

Cover Design: B.J. Graphics
Illustrations: Eric Lovstad
Typesetting by: AV Communications
Printed and Bound by: Bookcrafters, Inc.

10 9 8 7 6 5 4 3 2

Library of Congress Catalog Number: 94-69888
ISBN 1-885975-00-7: $17.95 US Dollars Softcover

# TABLE OF CONTENTS

For a more complete explanation and list of Dream Stones, Power Stones, Rescue Stones, and Shaman Stones, watch for Stone People's upcoming mineral reference books.

# DEDICATION

This book is dedicated to Dawn Lovstad, Charlotte Johnson, Kathryn Pinnella, Michael Marothey, Dixie McGuire, and our many, many other friends and supporters who have so freely and unhesitatingly given of their time, advice and unflinching encouragement. And of course to lovers of crystals everywhere.

Thanks. We wouldn't have kept at this without you.

## ABOUT THIS BOOK

*Crystal Personalities* is essentially a reference manual, specifically designed to equip you with instant identification of the forms quartz crystals take (known in the mineral world as their "habits") and the names they are most commonly called in our present time cycle.

All of this information was gleaned from extensive research into mineralogical, academic, and spiritual/metaphysical sources, as well as through personal experience and the presentation of workshops over the past five years. In addition to the books listed in our Bibliography, we have investigated many others in our attempt to gather as much information into one place as we can, up to the time of printing. We highly recommend each book in both the Bibliography and Additional Reading lists, but this in no way implies that these are the only books on minerals worth your time.

And this reference manual is not intended to be the final word on quartz crystal, the tasks it can perform, or its psychological-symbolic talents. We hope, in fact, that this one-stop information package only encourages you to trust your own personal responses to any one crystal, while at the same time alleviating the necessity of lengthy research on your own in places we have already been for you. This book by no means implies, however, that you should not do your own research.

We are confident that you will find additional crystal formations not yet recognized, the functions for which they were originally created, and the capacities inherent within them. There is in fact no reason why you should not be the one to write the next crystal best seller.

Remember that anything you experience when in the company of crystals is valid for *you*, and that your responses will always be highly individual and personal. And don't let anyone talk you out of your own experiences, not even us. There is no right or wrong way to feel. We guarantee that if you only use your crystals as mental and psychological reminders to focus on their symbolic meanings, you can't lose, and you will gain much insight into yourself.

Don't be discouraged if you can't find all of the crystals listed in this reference manual. Some of them are fairly rare and hard to find, and some, like Earthkeepers, would be too big to cart home anyway. (We know —we tried!). And thanks for helping us keep the research and information flowing by buying this book.

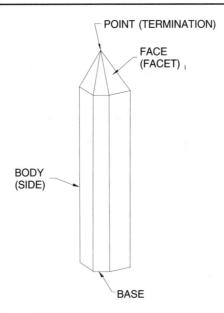

POINT (TERMINATION)

FACE (FACET)

BODY (SIDE)

BASE

## QUARTZ CRYSTAL: WHAT'S ALL THE FUSS ABOUT?

When most people talk about crystals they mean rock crystal, the most common form of quartz on our planet. This is the Grandfather of the Mineral Kingdom and many authorities estimate that as much as one-third of Earth's crust is made up of some type of quartz.

Physically, a quartz crystal is a solid material composed of silicon di-oxide (silica and oxygen) with a chemical formula of $SiO_2$. Quartz crystal belongs to the hexagonal crystal system and weighs 7 on the Mohs scale. Most quartz crystals are between 100 to 125 million years old, so treat these venerable ancients with the respect they deserve.

All quartz crystals have a precise regular hexagonal internal arrangement of atoms, often referred to as the *crystal spiral*. This spiral revolves either left or right and even mineralogists aren't sure why some spirals move one way and some the other, and frequently in the same quartz cluster. But it is this reliable arrangement of atoms which gives quartz crystals their priceless talents, both for crystal lovers and technology.

Clear quartz crystal may not be "clear" at all. It is often milky or snowy in appearance with visible or invisible inclusions of water, air, gases, or other minerals. But it will almost always be called clear in books about quartz crystal. Perfectly clear quartz crystal, however, is fairly hard to find in today's market and consequently continues to rise in price. Even insurance companies have begun to take note of its value.

Other members of the Quartz Crystal Clan are: Amethyst, Ametrine, Citrine, Rose Quartz, Snow or Milk Quartz, Smoky Quartz, Rutilated Quartz, Tourmalinated Quartz, all Agates, and all Jaspers. There is even a mineral called Jaspagate. But all of these Crystal Clan members will be listed in mineral books with a chemical formula of $SiO_2$, even though it is obvious they have inclusions of other minerals or substances. The good news about this is that every time you see the chemical formula $SiO_2$ connected with your stone, you know you are working with a form of quartz crystal, and all quartz crystal will behave the same at the quantum level.

## HOW DO THEY *DO* THAT?

So how do crystals work for and with you? In a much oversimplified explanation, the energy radiating from quartz crystal automatically resonates at the quantum level in harmony with human (and other) frequencies, in other words with human energy speeds.

Sound, color, and light are really just energy vibrating at different speeds. For instance, on the part of the color spectrum visible to human beings, the frequency or speed creating the color red vibrates the slowest and the frequencies of the color violet the fastest. And since the human body is, among other things, a large receiver (and has even developed specialized parts to receive and translate certain vibrations: eyes, ears, skin, nervous system, etc.), we can use the analogy of your brain as your tuner and your nervous system as your antennae. Crystals, then, can act as your satellite dishes, radar, amplifiers, CDs, and even computer networks. In other words, crystals naturally boost and extend your inherent powers in each of these analogical areas. In fact, the primary function of quartz crystal is to boost and amplify.

So when you hold a crystal for even a few brief seconds it begins to vibrate on a frequency in harmony with your physical body, and this harmonization extends to your mind. Think of them as members of a band or orchestra or choir. Different crystals play or add their own unique notes (frequencies), not the *same* notes you yourself play, but *harmonizing* notes which boost, amplify, condense, intensify, and dramatically spiff-up your own.

Crystal energy frequencies also have the inherent ability to support your efforts in surfacing information from your subconscious, information you already "know" on some level but stuff you are not consciously aware of at the moment for one reason or another, which we won't go into here.

Naturally terminated crystals are synchronized, are "in alignment", with the primal cosmic force, or life itself. In other words, quartz crystals are just naturally in harmony with the life force, even in its raw unformed state. The precise internal arrangement of quartz crystals we spoke of earlier ensures this constant and consistent harmony, and your crystals quite literally help you "stay in tune".

This is why holding a crystal, meditating with one, sleeping with one, or even just having them around you works so well. Your crystals continually automatically try to keep you in tune with their own harmonic synchronization with the primal energy of life, thereby keeping *you* more in harmony with life. It is important to remember that each crystal is a distinct individual with its own harmonic frequency oscillations, so, yes, it can make a difference which one you use when.

While crystals don't actually hold electrical charges of energy (in the way a battery does, for instance), each individual crystal when rubbed or squeezed does produce an electrical charge called *piezoelectricity* (*piezo* just means *applied pressure*). This is the talent of quartz crystal that has made it the darling of the technological crowd, including our own government. Crystals

3

in fact are so effective in technology they are now grown in environmentally-controlled laboratories to ensure that their structures are absolutely perfect.

But while crystals are first-rate conductors of almost any type of energy, they are very poor conductors of both heat and cold. This is the reason why crystals should never be exposed to rapid changes in temperature. For instance, don't place a cold crystal in hot water, or a warm one in cold water. Let your stone adjust to room temperature first. Crystals, like most minerals, are actually quite delicate and crack easily under many conditions, including extreme temperatures.

It is our firm belief, by the way, that chipped or otherwise "imperfect" crystals don't necessarily lose the qualities we have just been talking about. Some of our personal favorite and most useful crystals have been badly treated, either while being mined or after, and continue to flash some of the best rainbows and "feel" the best. We call these damaged crystals Warrior and Empathic Crystals (depending upon the extent of damage) and have found them exceptionally useful psychological reminders that getting some rough treatment in life neither lessens nor diminishes us. Often it is the bump or wound itself that allows the rainbow in the crystal to appear at all, making this kind of crystal a good reminder that we always have the power to do the same (see Rainbow Crystal). After all, if a mineral can do it, surely you can.

You should be aware that lead crystal is not actually quartz crystal at all but is glass mixed with lead. While lead crystal prisms refract light spectacularly, they will not have the qualities nor be capable of functioning like natural quartz crystal.

CRYSTAL SYMBOLISM

Stones have symbolized spiritual truth and even the Spirit itself from our earliest beginnings on this planet. Stones are also strong symbols of the human soul, of Spirit manifested within Matter, of inner growth, durability, and of knowledge made tangible or "solid".

Quartz crystals are ancient symbols for the Light of the Spirit (the Intellect of the Spirit). Crystals represent Truth received by the human mind as Truth is able to operate through the physical medium of the personality. They are extremely old symbols of self-illumination, perfect insight, and the passive aspect of the human will. Quartz crystal also symbolizes purity, clarity, the union of opposites (Spirit with Matter), and Truth on the Higher Mental Plan of Existence. And as if all of this weren't enough, crystals often share the symbolism of the Diamond, most likely because the ancients didn't often differentiate on the value between the two.

Naturally terminated quartz crystals symbolize the sum total of human evolution possible within the Third Dimension. The six sides of the crystal symbolize the six main energy centers of the body (the *Chakras*), the crystal's point or termination symbolizing the 7th Chakra, "that which connects with the Infinite". It is by mastery of the energies and lessons represented by the other six main Chakras that humanity is able to reach the 7th in its journey toward reconnection with its Source.

Kirlian photographs of quartz crystals show a white light radiating out from a blue star-like center, another good symbol on its own. And since each crystal is an individual, its Kirlian photograph is as distinctive to it as yours is to you. Experimentation with Kirlian photography and crystals also clearly shows that a crystal's energy patterns change as its environment changes, just one more thing crystals and humans have in common.

CHOOSING YOUR CRYSTAL

Our advice in choosing and using crystals is simply to follow your intuition, implicitly. All stones, including quartz crystals, are basically energy supplements. It's really not much more complicated than that and there is no mystical magical way to choose your crystal. And please keep your intellect out of it. If you want crystals to "make sense" to you, go study quantum physics and then come back to your crystals. In the meantime, try trusting your intuition.

CHECKING YOUR CRYSTAL'S ENERGY PATTERNS

Checking the energy flow and range of influence of your crystal is simple, and fun. Hold a pendulum (any weight on a 4-inch length of string or chain) approximately three to four inches above your crystal. Holding your hand perfectly still, allow the pendulum to move on its own. The first movement of your pendulum is tracking the primary energy layer of your crystal. Any subsequent movements by your pendulum is just showing you additional energy layers and how that energy moves outward from your stone. You should not be close to other stones, computers, microwaves, or TVS when checking the energy in your crystal as these will tend to disrupt the natural energy patterns and give you inaccurate readings.

As you experiment with your pendulum, you will discover that not all crystal points contain energy moving out through the point—sometimes the energy is completely circular or some other pattern. Similarly, not all crystal spheres have circular energy patterns—sometimes they are side-to-side or egg-shaped, or some other pattern.

You can use this same pendulum method to check the natural energy flow in just about anything, including your food. This is fun stuff, so don't miss trying it. If you get no movement from your pendulum, the most probable cause is your own beliefs stopping its movement, and you can even use *that* to prove to you how strong your mind actually is. And, no, we are not making any of this up. Try it.

WHAT CRYSTALS DO FOR YOU IF YOU DON'T GET IN THEIR WAY

It is our firm belief that one of the most valuable services performed for you by quartz crystals is to allow you to get in touch with, and trust, your natural intuition about what is appropriate and most beneficial in your personal growth process. They are exceptionally effective symbolic reminders at the psychological level to change your thinking or behavior in accordance with what that particular crystal symbolizes to you. For example, you might want to choose an Artemis Crystal when you want to remind yourself to aim straight at your target, or a Selene Crystal to remind you to pay attention to your "gut feelings" or intuition. Crystals and other minerals simply make things more visible and physical for you. Besides, they feel good.

Most crystal effects are extremely subtle and always highly experiential, so don't expect to necessarily get struck by a white flash or attain instant illumination every time you hold one. Their effects are often not long lasting because of this same subtlety. It takes approximately on average fifteen minutes for anything on you or within three feet of you to be absorbed by your physical body and its various energy layers, so don't be impatient if you don't feel anything instantly or dramatically. Any particularly strong reactions to a crystal are often just telling you that this is where your greatest energy deficiency is at that moment, and not that you are either a crystal avatar from Atlantis or spiritually deficient in some way (energy supplements, remember?).

Any strong counteracting thought or emotion you have, either consciously or subconsciously, will also distort or deflect altogether the crystal's actions. The good news about this is that gifts of crystals and other minerals is one of the few non-violative ways to help someone else. If that person's growth blueprint doesn't need or want the stone's energy patterns mingling with it, it will simply ignore, deflect, or override it altogether, with no harm done. But at least you'll know you tried, without being pushy.

Remember....anything you experience while in the company of your crystals is valid for you. Don't worry about what your best friend feels. You are an individual and so is each quartz crystal, so it is highly unlikely that any two people and any two crystals will ever interact in precisely the same way. And you will often experience different reactions to your own favorite crystals at different times since a crystal's energy patterns change with its environment, and so does yours.

So keep notes, believe in your natural intuitive talents and what you have already learned, and treat your crystals with as much respect as they give you. After all, you are just as likely to be on the cutting edge of new information as anyone else. The energy in crystals is real, but as with all things, your perception is your perception and not someone else's. Honor that at all times.

THE CARE AND FEEDING OF YOUR CRYSTALS

One of the most important things to remember about all minerals is that they are fragile. They chip, crack and break from just the mildest jolt or bump, just like fine antique china. The term *hardness* used by mineralologists is just a handy way of categorizing how hard one mineral is in relation to another, usually on what is called the Mohs scale. It has nothing whatsoever to do with how unbreakable or durable your stone is. *Hardness* in this context simply means that a stone registering 10 will scratch a 9, a 5 will scratch a 4, etc. Now, here are some of the basic Do's and Don'ts of crystal care and feeding:

•   Don't go near your crystals when you are depressed or furious. Crystals don't just boost and amplify "good" energy, they boost and amplify any energy. They are unable to discriminate and exceptionally sensitive to all energy frequencies. Crystals will amplify even your more unproductive feelings and thoughts right back at you, and anyone else unlucky enough to be within three feet of them. When you are experiencing either deep depression or anger, use some of your other stones (like Aragonite Twins or Lepidolite), not quartz

6

crystals. A possible exception to this Don't might be Smoky Quartz Crystal, but use your intuition on that one.

• Don't touch someone else's crystals without getting permission. Some people are extremely sensitive about this, and just because a crystal is in a highly visible place doesn't necessarily mean that it's okay to touch or handle it. Show respect—ask first.

• In general, don't let others handle the crystals you find yourself using most often, your "personal" crystals. When working with a crystal for a specific reason, it is important that both you and its frequencies interact and stay in harmony with as little other human frequencies intruding as possible. But, again, use your intuition on this one.

• NEVER expose Amethyst quartz crystal to direct sunlight for extended periods of time. The iron in Amethyst is unstable and the wonderful purple of Amethyst will fade and cannot be brought back.

• Don't expose your crystals to artificial lighting for long periods, particularly fluorescent lighting. The molecular structure of crystals can be damaged by the bending effects of unnatural light frequencies. Keep changing stones used decoratively in your home or office if they are exposed to fluorescent lighting, unless you can also regularly expose them to natural light. Sticking them in an office window won't work, however, since most glass in windows today purposely filters out ultraviolet rays. You will most likely find yourself naturally drawn to different crystals at different times anyway, so switching them around once in a while works well on several levels and keeps everyone happy and healthy.

• Don't ever place crystals on or near magnetic surfaces of any kind. Just like your computer floppies, your crystal's natural programs will be erased.

• Don't reuse any salt used in cleansing and recharging your crystals. The salt literally holds onto the old frequencies and will release them back into any new crystal or stone placed in the salt. (See page 8 for cleansing crystals).

• Wrap your crystals in soft materials when moving them, especially over long distances.

• Don't leave your crystals exposed to the sun in your car or other places, especially in summer. Not only are they likely to shatter or explode, they can start a fire from the concentrated sunlight magnified through the crystals.

• Don't leave your crystals where they can freeze. Any trapped air, water, gases, or other inclusions will often freeze and contract before the surrounding quartz, and your crystal may crack or even shatter. And, no, putting them in your freezer doesn't do anything good for them either.

CLEANING YOUR CRYSTALS

As you begin to trust your own intuitive feelings you will find that you always know exactly when and how to re-energize and cleanse your crystals and other minerals. Use any cleaning method that seems appropriate for the stone and the reason it needs to be cleared. There is no wrong or right way to do this and no method is superior to any other. It depends entirely on the crystal, its future use, what it already has been used for, or where it has been.

The general timeframe for leaving a crystal or stone in any cleansing or recharging process is from five minutes to three weeks, or longer. We personally have rarely found it necessary to cleanse any stone for longer than three days, but there will obviously be exceptions, especially for minerals used in alternative healing procedures.

As a general rule, soap should not be used on your crystals and they should never be rubbed with any abrasive materials. Most stones will scratch easily, and soap always leaves a film. And some minerals should never under any circumstances be cleaned with water since they will dissolve (e.g., Calcite, Halite, Selenite, etc). Now for some of the basic methods of revitalizing and cleansing your crystals:

◆ COMPADRES. Crystals and other minerals just love being around other crystals and minerals. Group your stones in different patterns, including setting them in and around plants and fresh growing herbs and flowers.

◆ COPPER. Pieces of copper are outstanding crystal recovery rooms. Copper is one of the best conductors of energy and recharges and energizes just about anything rapidly and efficiently. You can even create a crystal hospital of sorts by using a flat piece of copper and a copper pyramid.

◆ CRYSTAL CLUSTERS. Crystals and other minerals can be cleansed and recharged by just letting them rest on a Quartz Crystal Cluster. This is a good way to revitalize stones set in jewelry without damaging the metal.

◆ ESSENTIAL OILS. Rub your crystals with *pure* essential oils. Other stones can also be anointed with oil, but be sure you are dealing with a non-porous surface and that the oil won't soak into the stone and permanently stain it. Pure essential oils (operative word *pure*) are also beneficial in programming crystals; just choose the oil to suit your program.

◆ HEMATITE and PYRITE. Put your crystal on a piece of Hematite or Pyrite to clear, recharge, and ground it all at the same time. This is an especially good method when you've used your crystal in any kind of programming, including meditation and divination exercises.

◆ MOONLIGHT and STARLIGHT. It is widely believed that crystals and other minerals placed outside under the moon and star constellations are cleansed and energized and will store the frequencies from the moon and stars. It is probably best to place your crystals directly on the ground or on a natural bed of wood, sage, or even another mineral. Moonlight is frequently used when you want to program your crystal to boost your intuitive abilities, or for divinatory exercises, or to enhance Yin (feminine) qualities.

◆ RUNNING WATER. A quick fix when you are in a place where other methods aren't practical is to hold your crystal under cool, not cold, running water for a few seconds. This both cleanses and recharges it and is often all that is ever needed. Mineral books recommend purified water to clean most minerals, but use your intuition on that one. Again, remember not to clean soft porous or water-based minerals with water (Calcite, Halite, Selenite, etc).

◆ SALT. One of the most popular ways to cleanse stones is by covering them with salt crystals. Any type of salt crystals will do, and in our opinion does not have to be the more expensive sea salt. The salt crystals used to make ice cream are terrific for this and best of all, inexpensive. Put your crystal or mineral in a white ceramic dish (never use metal with salt) and pour enough salt to completely cover the stone. More than one stone at a time can be cleansed this way, but never reuse the salt after its done its job. And don't pour the used salt out the back door—the *devas* will get you if you do.

◆ SMUDGING. Smudge sticks should obviously always be used with extreme caution. Carefully light a smudge stick. When it has ignited, extinguish the flame by shaking it gently over a fireproof container or sink. Many people like to use large sea shells for this. It is only the smoke you want, not the flame. Move the smudge stick around yourself and the crystals or stones, making sure the stones actually pass through the smoke several times. A feather or fan can be used to help disperse the smoke evenly if you like. To extinguish the smudge stick, plunge the smoking end into sand or dirt. You can use water, but you will then have to let the smudge stick dry out completely before you can reuse it. BE ABSOLUTELY SURE THAT THE SMUDGE STICK IS COMPLETELY OUT before you walk away from it. They can continue to smolder for quite a while without you noticing it. AND NEVER THROW A SMUDGE STICK IN A WASTEBASKET, out or not. Remember that you are literally playing with fire, which demands a great deal of respect.

◆ SOUND. Crystals and other minerals can be programmed and recharged by sound. Music works well, but best of all is the sound of your own voice. Crystals are extraordinarily receptive to sound patterns, so remember that it is the tones and intensity of the tones that matters, not the words or human interpretations. Crystals don't really speak English, they just manage to work around it.

◆ SUNLIGHT. After all of our warnings about sunlight, yes, it is absolutely true that the sun can be used to recharge and cleanse crystals and other minerals. The key here is the length of time involved. In the summer or when the sun is particularly intense (like at high altitudes), it takes only seconds for a crystal to ignite a fire under the right conditions. Seconds, not minutes or hours. (This, however, is a very good thing if you are lost in the woods and need a fire). But too much sun can also cause your crystal or other mineral to crack or shatter. Even some crystals which look perfectly clear to the naked eye actually contain microscopic inclusions of air, water, gases, or other inclusions which will heat up and expand before the surrounding quartz.

Remember, you are always the best one to decide how and when to recharge or cleanse any crystal or mineral. Trust your intuition and get to know your crystals well enough to know when they need attention and a little TLC. They really aren't that different from you, you know.

POSSIBLE SIDE EFFECTS
In general, crystals and other minerals are just interesting energy vitamins, energy supplement sources. Sometimes you need more vitamin C, sometimes more E, and sometimes you need all of the antioxidants at once. You will always automatically be pulled to the crystal or mineral that can help round-out or tune-up your present energy fields, if you don't let your logical mind get in the way. (Threaten it with studying quantum physics if it doesn't chill out and we guarantee it will back down. The mind loves feeling logical, but it *hates* discipline).

While using minerals is really not much more complicated than trusting your own feelings, crystals and minerals obviously do much more for you and other living things than just filling in your energy blanks or gaps. But that is their primary benefit, and you really don't need to know much more about them than that for them to do their stuff.

Most people will never, ever experience any side effects of any kind at any time from wearing or using crystals or minerals. Any side effects that do arise are often nothing more complicated than the result of too much energy coming into your energy systems too rapidly. Your personal tolerance levels and energy requirements and balances are changing all of the time. Removing the crystal or stone from your body or immediate environment is almost always all that is needed to relieve any discomfort.

It's common, however, for any discomfort to last for several minutes until your energy adjusts or re-establishes its old patterns. Your body's energy patterns will always return to where they were once the stones are removed, usually within 20 minutes or less. As we said, crystal frequencies are exceptionally subtle in effect and consequently wear off fairly rapidly. If removing the crystal doesn't work for you fast enough, stand in running water for at least 20 minutes. This will thoroughly cleanse your physical body and its surrounding energies.

When you make a commitment to grow, when the real you begins to wake up, you will notice that you become more and more sensitive to all feelings and situations, especially anything that triggers highly emotional reactions. This is perfectly normal, and just like exercising unused muscles can make you a little stiff and sore the next day, re-establishing pathways to the real you can get your emotions a little sore. It is common to find yourself reacting emotionally out of all proportion to the actual event, for instance, always a dead giveaway that the situation causing your reaction is important to your overall growth and progress at the time. Understanding that there are no easy lazy ways to deal with this and that your workout equipment has been especially designed for you by one of your experienced trainers will help you begin to see your reactions as excellent personal workout equipment. Intensity is always a sure sign you've just bumped into an important piece of your own progress puzzle, probably even one you specifically wanted to work with this time around the Universe.

And each of us insists in lugging around old, unproductive beliefs, feelings and thought patterns that should be regularly overhauled as part of our personal maintenance. Crystals and other minerals are one of the fastest ways to begin to help surface this outdated subconscious material. They then go on about their business of helping you work with, upgrade, or toss out this now unproductive useless baggage altogether. Just remember to never stuff any feeling or deny that you don't have it or that you should be beyond it by now. This all too human tendency is what got most of us in trouble in the first place. Remember…there are no mistakes, only learning experiences.

While most of us will never experience any side effects from crystals or minerals, if you or anyone you know should, here are some of the more common symptoms to watch for:

▶ ANGER or DEPRESSION. When you begin the process of conscious growth, it is not uncommon to experience inexplicable times when you feel like crying for no apparent reason whatsoever. Equally common are the times when you are furiously frustrated, or angry out of all proportion to the actual situation. These experiences will be magnified if you are enhancing your growth process with crystals or other minerals. If fact, this is the primary reason most of us get involved with crystals to begin with. It's important to keep in mind during these times that these emotions are *not* negative. And they aren't new. You've always had them, you just had them stuffed in the back of your emotional closet or buried deep inside your subconscious trunk. Think of these feelings as your own spiritual aerobic workout equipment, and let yourself experience the emotions from this new perspective (feeling them doesn't, however, mean you have to spew them all over the people around you). If your best friend were having any of these feelings, what would you tell him or her? Denying the feelings are there only puts them back on your emotional shelf and you can be sure that they will pop out at the most inconvenient and inappropriate times in the future. Not to mention that stuffing your feelings eventually makes you very, very sick. These feelings have come to your attention for a reason, and if you weren't ready to work with them, they wouldn't have come forward. Trust, remember?

► HEADACHES. Any headaches caused from crystals or other minerals almost always show up in the center of the forehead and most often feel like a sinus or "ice cream" headache. This one will have a sharper, "cleaner" feel, however, and is nothing more than a stimulation and clearing of the intuitive portion of your mind, or your "third eye" center. Just remove the stone from your body or environment, and begin to build your tolerance level more slowly by using smaller stones for shorter periods of time.

► HEAT or COLD. Body temperatures can fluctuate when wearing, handling, or just hanging around crystals and other minerals, very much as it shifts during meditative or other altered states of consciousness. HEAT generally indicates that energy is entering your system. COLD generally means that energy is leaving, usually fairly rapidly. If either of these sensations become too uncomfortable, simply remove the stone and allow your tolerance levels to build more slowly by using smaller pieces over shorter periods of time.

► LIGHTHEADEDNESS. This is a common experience after alternative healing or balancing procedures. Again, it signals a change in energy and consciousness. Mild dizziness or a feeling of being lightheaded or weak-kneed can also simply mean that you are being exposed to too many crystals or minerals at one time for too long a period. You may feel that you are "in a different place" (which you are) or have a feeling of being distanced from your normal feelings about your reality (and you temporarily are). This altered state passes very quickly as you adjust to the new frequencies coming into your system. Again, if these feelings are too uncomfortable, just remove the stones from your body or proximity. Eat or drink something with sugar in it or physically carry out a normal everyday task to speed up the process. If these symptoms show up every time you are around crystals, just learn to pace yourself. It doesn't mean there is something wrong with you or that you are resisting change. You gain nothing at all by trying to grow too fast, by trying to push the river. All you'll end up with is a bad case of spiritual indigestion and windburn.

► NAUSEA and/or DIARRHEA. Either of these symptoms is exceptionally rare, but overexposure to quartz crystal and other minerals has been known to cause them in some people. If you experience either of these symptoms, the most likely cause is the size of your stone. Down-size it till you find which frequency your physical body can best tolerate at the time. For example, if you want to work with a Generator Crystal, just use a smaller one. It doesn't mean you can't work with Generators. Either of these symptoms just indicates that at that time you are extraordinarily sensitive to the frequency interchanges taking place. In most cases, a week or less of slowly increasing your exposure time allows your energy systems to comfortably unwind any knots or blocks of energy causing these side effects. Always remember that you are the one in charge, *you* set the pace and make the rules. There is no contest to see who expands consciousness first.

▶ NUMBNESS. If your fingers, toes, hands, feet, or nose develop a feeling of slight numbness, it is probably just caused by the electromagnetic resonance between you and the crystal. Remove the stone and build your tolerance.

▶ SHOOTING PAINS. If you find that you are so sensitive to a particular crystal or combination of them that you experience mild stabbing pains in some area of your body (an exceptionally rare symptom), it is usually a sign that you are for some reason just absorbing too much energy too fast. Remove the stone or stones and build your tolerance levels more slowly.

▶ MILD PRICKLING. Sometimes you will feel tiny electric-like shocks similar to the feeling you get when your hand or foot "falls asleep". In this case, however, the tingling sensation is caused by a change in energy flow rather than blood flow. Under normal conditions, these feelings last only a few minutes or seconds and are not really uncomfortable, just "tingly". In deep meditation these same sensations are often called the "tickling of the ant". Energy tingles will most often affect the part or parts of your body which have suffered some kind of trauma or damage (physical and psychological) to its natural energy flow. Your crystals are just trying to iron out the rough spots, but if you are uncomfortable, remove the stones and work with smaller ones.

Again, remember that most of us never experience any of these side effects. But if you do, your sensations are all perfectly normal and they neither indicate that you are on a particularly "high" spiritual or growth level nor a "low" one (whatever that means). Any reactions to crystals and other minerals is quite physical and caused by nothing more than an exchange of energies, but you aren't imagining them. They *are* real.

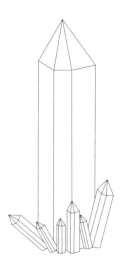

ABUNDANCE CRYSTAL

An Abundance Crystal is a crystal with individual smaller crystals clustered at or around its base or sprinkled along one or more of its sides. Abundance Crystals are symbolic of the abundance and profusion of the things in your life already within easy reach, maybe even just at your feet waiting for you to wake up and notice them. Abundance Crystals remind you to recognize this abundance for what it is and what it can help you do, and most of all to realize that it is already supporting and sustaining you.

Meditation with or focusing on an Abundance Crystal helps you become more comfortable with your personal beliefs about abundance, prosperity, affluence, and wealth in all of their forms. Once you truly grasp this feeling, abundance is literally only a thought away. These crystals help you begin to attract what is in reality already yours, you have just forgotten to ask for it clearly and precisely. Abundance Crystals are strong symbols that you are limited only by your own beliefs about what you deserve and are allowed to have. Remember one of the basic laws of physics—like attracts like. *Feel* abundant and it is already 80% yours and moving closer with each thought. How would you walk, talk, stand, sit differently if you had the abundance you want right now? *Do it.* (This does not mean that you run around charging up all of your plastic to the brim. That isn't abundance, it's using someone else's money, with interest).

So Abundance Crystals are good choices for programming to bring more abundance into your life. But first get quite clear about what you believe abundance is. Is it money, energy, health, love, friends, all of the above and more? *Put it in writing.* If you can't, you still aren't clear about what you believe abundance to be. What would it take to make you feel abundant? How would abundance change your life? How would you have to change your present behavior to have abundance? Does that please, or displease, you? Is there any part of this feeling that frightens some other part of you, and if so, is it causing you to send out mixed signals about having abundance? And if you have just discovered that you don't know what abundance really means to you, you at least now have some idea of why you don't have it. If you don't know, who does?

This crystal is also an outstanding protection stone, symbolizing the parent or guardian protecting and supporting its little ones. Abundance Crystals remind you to protect and support your own ideas and dreams and to act on them step-by-step with child-like trust. They are constant reminders that you are supported in all that you do at all times, that you are never alone, and that there are constantly new parts of you with new experiences coming into awareness to help you reach your goals. (See also Crystal Cluster).

ABUNDANCE CRYSTAL QUICK REFERENCE:

Symbolizes your natural power and ability to create what you want.
One of the Power Stones.
One of the Rescue Stones.
A good Dream Stone.
Focuses your attention on prosperity and abundance.
Helps attract abundance of all kinds.
Promotes lighter, happier attitudes.
Keeps reminding you to act on your dreams with trust.
Reminds you that there is always more coming.
Excellent choice to erase "I can't do it" thoughts and feelings.
Helps you deal with deep inner fears of failing.
First rate depression fighter.
Excellent energy recharger.
Outstanding choice for business people and entrepreneurs.
Stimulates feelings of compassion toward those less gifted.
Good choice for attaining harmony in your life at all levels.
Promotes a stronger desire for freedom and independence.
Stimulates feelings of safety and security by remembering you have support.
Helps you deal with fear of your personal power to create what you want.
Aids you in communicating more directly with your Higher or Inner Self.
A good tool for generating a desire for empathy and cooperation with others.
Stores unlimited potential for growth through your conscious cooperation
        and support by and of others.

ARTEMIS CRYSTAL

A long crystal with a sharp undamaged point is an Artemis Crystal. An Artemis resembles an arrow and is really just an elongated Generator Crystal. Artemis Crystals are sometimes called Diana Crystals. They are often mistaken for Laser Wand Crystals, but a Laser resembles a finger more than an arrow.

Artemis was the Goddess of the Hunt, Goddess of the Moon, and champion and protectress of women, children, wild creatures, sacred groves, and all wilderness areas. Sacred groves were under the protection of Artemis and her predecessor goddesses. Artemis was one of the many faces or characteristics of the Mother God or Divine Mother and often addressed as Queen of Heaven, Mother of All Creatures, the Triple Goddess, the Great She-Bear (the Ursa Major pole star), the Mother of Mercy, and Heart of the World. Artemis is the big sister many of us have never had. The worship and veneration of Artemis in some form has been traced back in our present time cycle to Neolithic times.

Artemis Crystals arouse your own innate feelings of independence, freedom, and the unshakable desire to be more self-sufficient. They are especially useful for those of us trying to become an autonomous individual at any level—economically, spiritually, creatively, emotionally, mentally, physically,—since Artemis has always been a special champion of those trapped, imprisoned, and rendered defenseless by external forces.

Artemis Crystals are the archers of the Crystal Clan, the masters of the hunt. Thoughts, prayers, wishes, and affirmations sent through these crystals zoom unerringly to the target. They are outstanding protection stones and help you learn to work with and overcome unreasonable anxieties and fears, especially fear of doing things on your own or without the support of male (Yang) energies.

Choose an Artemis any time you need to focus your thoughts and any time you need a quick physical or mental energy fix. Artemis Crystals are also good reminders of the inner knowledge and wisdom born within each of us, a contact point to help you reach back to your true origin and begin the process of remembering.

An Artemis is an excellent gift for anyone involved in any way with the process of childbirth (real or symbolic) and anyone reaching for freedom, independence, and personal identity.

ARTEMIS CRYSTAL QUICK REFERENCE:

Symbolizes Wisdom and Mercy.
Represents Artemis as Mother of All Creatures.
Symbolizes strength, courage, independence, and competition.
The Archer of the Crystal Clan.
One of the best Rescue Stones.
Stimulates a strong desire for and feelings of personal freedom.
Helps you fight and overcome unnecessary fears and anxieties.
First rate protection stone.
Reminds you to keep your eye unwaveringly on your target.
Dissipates excessive or inappropriate physical and material longings.
Superior channelling tool.
Disrupts and breaks up old unproductive patterns of addiction.
Reawakens your desire for the Real in your life, shooting down illusion.
Helps you work with fear of your personal power to create solely on your own.
A good aid in any decision-making process.
Stimulates feelings of courage and determination.
A good tool for communicating with teachers, visible and invisible.
Balances Yin-Yang (female-male) energies and qualities.
Excellent choice for business people and entrepreneurs.
Strongly recommended for hunters of all kinds.
Strengthens your belief in your style of personal creativity.
A good psychic energy stone.
Outstanding telepathic communication stone.
Recommended for pregnant and nursing mothers.
Highly recommended for anyone working with any aspect of childbirth.
Symbolizes the Triple Goddess in her roles of Young Girl, Mature Woman,
     and Wise Old Woman or Crone.
Outstanding choice for affirmations and prayers, sending your
     thoughts and feelings unerringly to their targets.
Symbolizes the Mother God as the Heart of the World, Queen of Heaven,
     Mother of Mercy, Nurturer of All.

CATHEDRAL CRYSTAL

A Cathedral Crystal is a crystal that has no upper dividing line between the facet and one of its sides which create its point (termination). In other words, a Cathedral has two long straight lines forming one of its sides but only two lines forming that side's part of the point. This is a relatively rare formation for a crystal to achieve and is often found as the opposite side of the receiver face of a Receiver Crystal.

The ancient Etruscans divided Heaven into two straight lines which intersected at a point directly overhead. The point symbolized the Center of the Universe, and the two lines represented the North-South and East-West Planes of Existence. Psychic and spiritual phenomena occurring within this area were interpreted according to their position in relation to this "cathedral" space. This space was an area of sacred revelations, where intercommunication between the Three Worlds (Upper, Terrestrial, and Lower) could take place. You can use your Cathedral Crystal in exactly the same way, making this an exceptional channelling tool.

Symbolically, a cathedral or temple represents the Inner Mind or Inner Self as it spiritually takes form within physical matter. Cathedrals are places of renewal for the human spirit, places especially created for and dedicated to focus on the sacred and divine. Your Cathedral Crystal reminds you to maintain this connection yourself, and that you are always safely tucked inside your own sanctuary, that nothing can ever really harm you unless you believe it can. The real you can never be threatened.

The combination Cathedral Crystal and a Receiver Crystal face on the same stone boosts and enhances your ability to connect directly with Spirit (however you personally translate that), and allows you to then bring back with you into your everyday life the nourishment and renewal you require at that moment. If you want to make practical use of this information, try pairing your Cathedral with a piece of Fluorite.

CATHEDRAL CRYSTAL QUICK REFERENCE:

Symbolizes the communication between Heaven and Earth.
Symbolizes your constant connection to the Infinite, the Sacred, the Divine.
First rate Dream Stone.
Excellent Rescue Stone
Helps you fight depression and feelings of "what's the use?"
Outstanding divination tool.
Especially good choice when working with any ego-related issues.
Matchless telepathic communication tool.
Great comforter during times of transition and change.
Generates feelings of peace, serenity, and trust.
Takes an active part in transformations of any kind.
Helps you create a sanctuary-like atmosphere anytime, anywhere.
Enhances your spiritual attunement at all levels of existence.
Outstanding meditation tool.
Helps you learn patience, tolerance, compassion, and unconditional love.
Good tool for communicating with the Higher and Inner Self.
First rate channelling tool.
Reminds you that you are a spiritual being having a human experience.
Excellent choice to attain and maintain spiritual attunement and balance.
Assists you in seeing through your spiritual eyes as well as your human ones.
Helps you deal with anxieties caused primarily by feelings of not being
        connected to or having forgotten your true Self.

## CHANNELLING CRYSTAL

A Channelling Crystal is a crystal with seven lines making up the outline of one its faces (facets), with a perfect triangle *directly opposite* this 7-sided face. This is the Sage of the Crystal Clan, a stone for scientists and seekers, those who want to know why and how, and how to then act on this information with intelligence. A Channelling Crystal is also sometimes called a Spiritual Growth Crystal or a 7-Sided Crystal.

The 7-sided face symbolizes the seven qualities human consciousness must master to access the wisdom of the Total Self: (1) Love, (2) Knowledge, (3) Bliss, (4) Freedom, (5) Peace, (6) Manifestation, and (7) Unity. For this reason, the 7-sided face also symbolizes the Spiritual Seeker, the Mystic Student, one who has dedicated herself or himself to discovering their true nature and relationship to the One.

The 3-sided face of the triangle on the Channelling Crystal symbolizes the integration of body, mind, and spirit as they connect with and strengthen the Seeker (the 7-sided face).

This crystal also symbolizes the numbers 7 and 3, each a strong symbol in its own right. Seven symbolizes (among many other things) a new beginning after the completion of a cycle; the completion of your former state or level of development; the four Earth elements (often represented by a square) combining with Spirit (often represented by a circle); and has always been viewed as a particularly healing number. The number seven also symbolizes Perfect Order (4+3); Heaven over Earth; the normal cycles of growth; the Great Mother; secret or hidden knowledge; Celestial Harmony; virginity; and the Nucleus of All That Exists. The number seven was sacred to several deities, including Apollo, Ares, Artemis, and Osiris.

The number three symbolizes any trinity or triad, a gathering together of spiritual forces (often represented by a triangle); and the process of obtaining perfection while still within Matter (often represented by a triangle within a square). Three also symbolizes creative power through unity; growth; forward and upward movement; synthesis; multiplicity; and the ability to speak Absolute Truth.

Together, the 7 and 3 of your Channelling Crystal add up to the number 10 (7+3), the number of completion which leads you back again to the number 1 and the beginning of a new slightly higher turn on the spiral of your continuing journey.

A Channelling Crystal is an excellent stone to place in a chaotic or disruptive atmosphere since being close to one automatically stimulates the consciousness of anyone in its immediate vicinity and promotes a stronger desire for truthfulness, serenity, harmony, and the subconscious desire to get back on track with the true purpose of any meeting, to do what you came to do.

A Channelling Crystal helps you attain conscious connection to the ultimate source of your own accumulated knowledge and wisdom, allowing you to better "channel" information from You to you. Use this crystal as a booster or fine-tuner to align you to your Higher and Inner Self, and then beyond.

Meditation with a Channelling Crystal can keep you in line with your spiritual goals and help you check your progress along your way. This crystal should probably be one of your personal stones and kept away from other people, but use your intuition on that one.

CHANNELLING CRYSTAL QUICK REFERENCE:

Symbolizes the Spiritual Seeker, the Mystic Student.
Symbolizes Spirit perfecting itself within Matter.
Symbolizes the Seven Cosmic Stages of spiritual development.
Represents the Seven Celestial Tones and Seven Celestial Spheres.
Symbolizes the integration of Body, Mind, and Spirit as linked to the Seeker.
The Sage of the Crystal Clan.
One of the true channelling stones (as is a Kyanite blade).
Helps you align more directly to your Higher Self and maintain that alignment.
Stimulates a strong desire for wisdom and integration with the One.
Generates a desire for truthfulness, especially with yourself.
Excellent energy shield.
Boosts any and all consciousness within its immediate environment.
Represents the seven qualities human consciousness must attain
        and master in order to access the Total Self.
Activates and connects the 4th, 5th, 6th, 7th, 8th, 9th,
        10th, 11th, and 12th chakras.

COMET CRYSTAL

Comet Crystals are crystals with a number of tiny crater-like indentations on one or more sides of the crystal ending in a spray trailing behind, resembling the tail of a comet.

Comet Crystals magnify your capacity to discover and maintain a more realistic sense of your world and your place in it. Meditating or sleeping with a Comet Crystal is a great way to reawaken your understanding of what is often meant by "cosmic consciousness", of getting in sync with the entire universe, seeing or remembering the "big picture". Comet Crystals also remind you that nothing in the Universe stands still or can ever remain exactly the same or unchanged for very long, and that things are not always what they appear to be from a distance.

Comets are made of fire, ice, and light, and great symbols in their own right. They are strong representations of tremendous creative power and energy, transformation, and cyclic but rapid change. A comet has almost always been seen as a messenger, a bringer of either good fortune or of strong warnings. What they are made up of at their point of origin is definitely not what they are after several trips around our galaxy—just like you. Your Comet Crystal can stimulate your own natural psychic awareness so you can decipher your incoming information more clearly and accurately.

COMET CRYSTAL QUICK REFERENCE:

Symbolizes the Fire of Spirit transforming the ice of human complacency.
Symbolizes tremendous power and energy rushing at you from above.
Represents swift movement, literally burning up the skies.

COMET CRYSTAL Continued:

Helps activate your natural psychic awareness.
Stimulates tremendous creative energies.
Reminds you to accept being physical on planet Earth.
Aids in understanding what is meant by Universal or Cosmic Consciousness.
Stimulates sluggish energy patterns.
A good telepathic communication tool.
Helps you come to terms with your personal power and your use of it.
First rate energy recharger.
Good reminder that what goes around always comes back around.
Helps in making long-term decisions.
Reminds you of the cyclic nature of all things.
Good choice during times of rebirth, transition, or transformation.
Helps you find your particular place within your own universe.
A good reminder that nothing can remain unchanged or the same forever.
Reminds you that you keep changing as you move forward, and the faster
        you move, the more you change.

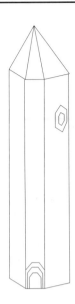

CRATER CRYSTAL

A Crater Crystal is a crystal that at one time had one or more other crystals growing attached to one or more of its sides or its base. The now-missing crystal(s) has left behind it a crater-like depression.

Craters symbolize your capacity to detach, let go, and still keep on growing as an individual, even with someone or something important missing from your life. Crater Crystals are also excellent symbols of the child who has left home, no longer requiring the parent to support it or give it form, protection, or a framework on which to grow.

Craters are good reminders to release your attachment to almost anything, making this a good birthing and rebirthing tool and a good choice when working with addictions of all kinds.

Crater Crystals also remind you of the multiple characteristics of the Whole Self, and that all things must inevitably let go or be let go. As you've probably guessed by now, Craters are outstanding when working with lessons of non-attachment and letting go.

Craters are good symbol substitutes for cups, and both cups and craters are ancient symbols of the World-Soul as the vehicle of the Higher Self. They are both used symbolically to remind us that the individual Soul springs from the World-Soul and is constantly filled, refreshed, and nourished by its Higher Self.

Since geophysical craters are formed by swift, violent impacts, a Crater Crystal is also a good reminder that you don't want to wait until you get hammered by your outside environment to get the point.

CRATER CRYSTAL QUICK REFERENCE:

Symbolizes the World-Soul as the vehicle for the individual Soul.
Represents your ability to let go and still remain whole.
Symbolizes the child or student who has left the nest.
Excellent choice when working with martyrdom and "poor me" lessons.
Recommended for both students and teachers.
Outstanding choice for parents and children.
A good choice for working with addictions of any kind.
Helps you learn to get the point *before* you get hammered.
Good birthing and rebirthing tool.
Excellent choice during transitions and change.
Good reminder of the multiplicity of the Whole Self.
Excellent choice for any personal inner work.
One of the best for working with non-attachment lessons.
Reminds you to support and nurture always, and then *let go*.
Reminds you that you have the capacity to continue to grow
        on your own without the constant support of others.

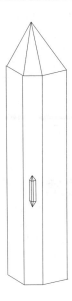

CREATOR CRYSTAL

A Creator Crystal is a larger crystal with a tiny, *completely formed* crystal buried deep within it. A Creator Crystal is not an Inner Child or a Phantom Crystal, but a highly specialized, rarer crystal formation (see Inner Child Crystal and Phantom Crystal).

Creator Crystals are outstanding points of focus when you are creating new forms and for visualizing anything at all you want to bring into your life. Focusing on a Creator Crystal reminds you that there is always a seed of creativity, new energy, and spirit inside of you just waiting to be noticed and given birth.

Creator Crystals are reminders of the master teacher or god-in-embryo within you whose only desire and purpose is to be consciously awakened. These crystals, of course, make superior meditation and dream tools and are highly effective in crystal layout and programming patterns.

CREATOR CRYSTAL QUICK REFERENCE:

Symbolizes "that which is coming forth."
Represents fertility in all of its aspects.
One of the Shaman Stones.
Outstanding Dream Stone.
Excellent meditation and visualization tool.
Dramatically enhances all forms of creativity.
Stimulates a strong desire to bring your daydreams into practical reality.
A good divination tool.
Excellent tool during creative transformation procedures.

CREATOR CRYSTAL continued:

Actively stimulates psychic and spiritual awakening.
Stimulates and enhances fertility on all levels.
A good tool for finding your pre-birth purpose.
Good choice during past-life and parallel life recall procedures.
Reminds you that you are always creating new growth.
Reminds you of the master teacher within.
Excellent choice for programming.
Superior visualization tool.
Highly recommended for entrepreneurs of all kinds.
Reminds you that you are always in a state of becoming,
       that you are not yet a finished product.

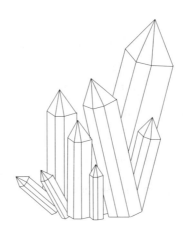

CRYSTAL CLUSTER

Crystal Clusters symbolize individuals living together in harmony and cooperation, leaning on and trusting one another for support. Clusters also symbolize peace, family, optimum results through combined energy, and the Universe with its multiple parts. (In the mineral world two or more crystals growing together technically constitute a cluster).

Crystal Clusters are excellent choices to place in areas where individuals regularly meet and need to cooperate with one another. They are especially valuable for stimulating a desire for effective communication, which automatically leads to more productive relationships. Position any variety of Crystal Cluster (Amethyst, Smoky, Clear, Rutilated, etc.) in a corner of any room where you would like to change and harmonize what's happening in the room. They are outstanding energy shields as well, especially Smoky or Tourmalinated Clusters.

Just as in any family, each crystal in a Cluster is a distinct individual, so examine your Crystal Cluster to find the many crystal personalities living there. The size of your cluster does not necessarily indicate its energy range or strength so be sure to investigate its energy movements (see page 5).

Small Crystal Clusters are outstanding at energizing the energy centers of the physical body (the chakras). Clusters in general help to keep all life forms energized and clear of any heavy, slow-moving, unproductive energy.

CRYSTAL CLUSTER QUICK REFERENCE:

Symbolizes cooperation and harmony between dissimilar individuals.
Represents individuals grouped together for maximum results.
Actively and dramatically stimulates and boosts creativity.
Generates the desire to cooperate and harmonize with others.
Boosts communication capacities at all energy levels.
Equalizes and stabilizes most energies in its immediate environment.
Dissipates depression and heavy, unproductive thoughts.
Good choice anywhere compatibility and communication are essential.
Boosts and enhances psychic energy.
Very good choice for naturally shy people.
Excellent psychic energy protection.
Excellent choice for thought and other energy amplification.
Beneficial for all of the human chakras.
Great tool for attaining mental and emotional equilibrium.
Balances both Yin (female) and Yang (male) energies.
Outstanding energy shield.
Helps you deal with normal, everyday insecurities and anxieties.
First rate booster of physical energy levels.
Natural energy cleanser of its immediate environment.
Cleanses and energizes other stones, rooms, people, and all living things.
Symbolizes individuals cooperating with one another to form
        a single unit for a specific purpose or process.

## CRYSTAL SPHERE

Crystal Spheres have been favorites of ours for thousands of years, especially when it comes to *scrying*, seeing into the present, future, and past.

All spheres are crystal circles, and circles symbolize among other things: Totality; Wholeness; Original Perfection; the Self; Eternity; Infinity; Celestial Unity; the Unmanifest; Unconditional Love; spiritual attunement; completeness; serenity; all cycles; the sun, moon, planets and all other celestial bodies; endless movement with no beginning and no ending; Time surrounding and enclosing Space; a return to the Whole Self; Perfect Order—and we've barely put a dent in the possible interpretations of circle. Even the circumference of your Crystal Sphere has its own symbolism, representing all cyclic movements; the precise and regular boundaries of the world of form; the inner unity of all Matter; Universal Harmony; and human growth, destiny, and evolution.

You might like to use a small Crystal Sphere to remind you of your tremendous potential for growth and the lessons you will master through that growth, and a larger Sphere to remind you of the power of spiritual and Universal love, and that there is always room for everyone and everything to be held within that circle of Unconditional Love.

Spheres also represent the number 10, an important symbol on its own. Ten, among other things, is the symbol for the Cosmos, the All, the Unity, the totality of the Universe, Absolute Perfection. It is the number of completion since all numbers ultimately return to 1. Ten represents the all-inclusive and tells you that all things are possible. Ten symbolizes the completion of journeys, the successful completion of the spiritual Initiate, but can also represent the recommencement of a series or cycle since it 10 represents the circle enclosing itself. It is often used to symbolize a marriage.

The energies in a Crystal Sphere usually spin rapidly within the circular shape of the Sphere, radiating outward in the same pattern formed when you drop something into water. But be sure to check the energy flow of your Crystal Sphere first (see page 5). Not all Spheres have this circular energy pattern, but instead function more like a crystal point or some other pattern.

The precise circular action emitted by most Crystal Spheres, however, makes it an especially good candidate for programming since your program will be broadcast in precise, regular, circular waves moving farther and farther out in continuously widening circles.

And, as with all of your crystals, don't forget to check your Spheres for phantoms or other specialized forms. Many of them are also Selene Crystals, Teacher Crystals, Devic Crystals, and even Phantoms, and a good reminder that there is rarely just one answer or interpretation of anything, or just one way to use it effectively.

CRYSTAL SPHERE QUICK REFERENCE:

Symbolizes the Whole or Total Self.
Symbolizes Original Perfection and Eternity.
An ancient symbol for the number 10 with all of its interpretations.
Symbolizes Time enclosing and surrounding Space.
Represents Spiritual Attunement and Completeness, the All That Is.
Symbolizes Unconditional Love and Perfect Harmony.
One of the Shaman Stones.
One of the primary geometric shapes.
Stimulates the continual desire for harmony and peace.
Actively stimulates creativity.
First rate choice for maintaining spiritual balance and connection.
Excellent general communication tool.
Effective tool when working with mental and emotional imbalances.
Carries a long history for use in divination and scrying exercises.
Dramatically enhances your natural intuitive powers.
Helps fight melancholy and depression.
Awakens and boosts your natural psychic abilities.
Excellent choice for teachers.
Stimulates a strong desire for self-awareness and personal growth.
Amplifies thought, feelings, and other energies.
Outstanding choice for programming.
Helps soothe nervousness and anxieties.
First rate meditation tool.
Excellent tool for concentration and focus.
Good aid for uncovering your belief systems.
Excellent telepathic communication tool.
Good choice for communication with "higher" energies.
Good choice for communication with your Higher Self.
Reminds you of your enormous, unending potential for growth.
Excellent reminder that there is always room for more.

DEVIC CRYSTAL

A Devic Crystal is a crystal with multiple internal fractures and inclu-sions of trapped water, air, and gases. Devic Crystals can be any shape, vari-ety of quartz crystal, formation, or size and do not have to have perfect termi-nations or even any termination at all.

The trapped water, air, or gas within your Devic Crystal is often called *veils* and *fairy frost*. It was once widely believed that fairies and other nature spirits stayed in these crystals as they travelled from one place to another, turning a Devic Crystal at one level into a kind of hostel for nature spirits.

A Devic Crystal helps you become more open to the possibility that Earth does indeed have "nature spirits". Once you have proven that you can be trusted to be a caretaker of this planet and its life forms, these protectors of Earth may communicate with you through your Devic Crystal. If you earn the trust of these energies, they will teach you a great deal about the true nature of this planet and its function in our Universe. And if you are very, very good they might even take you to visit the inner realms of planet Earth, or the king-doms behind the mists.

*Devas* themselves are light beings assigned to planet Earth to assist her various life forms and energies. Throughout human history, Devas have been elves, fairies, and other nature spirits, although Devas in the oldest exist-ing legends were believed to be what we now call angels. The Sanskrit root word *devi* itself translates as *goddess*. So your Devic Crystal is a reminder of your own supra-normal powers of consciousness and your natural ability to reconnect with "beings of light". This crystal is a wonderful gift for any newborn anything since devas and fairies like to bring extraordinary and miraculous gifts to infants. And Devic Crystals are, of course, great for plants of all kinds.

DEVIC CRYSTAL QUICK REFERENCE:

Symbolizes the supra-normal powers of your own consciousness.
Helps you accept being physical here on planet Earth.
One of the best tool for communicating with "the little people."
Useful as a telepathic communication tool.
Great comforter when working with physical fears of all kinds.
Excellent psychic energy generator and tool.
Connects directly with Earth's attending spirits and energies.
A good tool for discovering Earth's place and function in the Universe.
Stimulates compassion and understanding for all life forms.
Outstanding gift for the newly born.
Good tool for staying in touch with Earth changes.
Helps you become aware of and more in tune with the problems
        facing this planet.

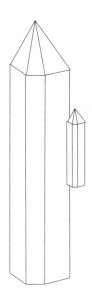

DOLPHIN CRYSTAL

A Dolphin Crystal is one large crystal with a much smaller, shorter crystal fastened securely to its side. Dolphins are not Soul Mates or Twin Flames (see Soul Mate Crystal, Twin Flame Crystal).

Dolphin Crystals symbolize your natural craving and right to be cherished, nurtured, and appreciated just the way you are. Dolphins remind you of your innate capacity to provide this same atmosphere for yourself as well as others. This is an excellent choice anytime you feel particularly insecure and in need of the security of a good companion, especially when you are about to go swimming in deep waters. Dolphins also remind you that making someone else feel safe, wanted, and cherished is one of the best ways to receive the same energies yourself. (Like attracts like, remember?)

Dolphin Crystals provide first rate protection for the newly born, the young, defenseless, gentle, sensitive, naive, and the innocent. They are exceptional at reducing anxiety, deep fear, and anger. Dolphins remind you to stay in touch with your playful, fun loving, carefree nature, to not take things so seriously all of the time.

Meditating or sleeping with a Dolphin can help you become better attuned to the water dwellers of this planet, as well as your own compassionate, sensitive, intuitive nature (*yes, you do!*)

Dolphin Crystals are good choices for people who need to reawaken their capacity to give emotional support and understanding to themselves as well as others, and to re-learn how to accept this support without feeling weak, defenseless, or vulnerable.

Dolphins make good dream stones and promote sound, restful sleep; a good choice to keep away nightmares and things that go bump in the night, especially if it's a Smoky Quartz Dolphin Crystal.

Symbolically, the dolphin is a strong savior symbol, especially for anyone in danger of shipwreck, smashing themselves on the rocks. The dolphin is the king of fishes and sacred to all ancient sea deities, male and female. Dolphins were also one of the Guides of the Soul (a Psychopomp), and a strong symbol of the Soul's journey across the Sea of Death. Dolphins also represent swiftness, intelligence, safety, knowledge, and the power and intelligence of the sea or the deep and unfathomable.

DOLPHIN CRYSTAL QUICK REFERENCE:

Symbolizes safety when moving through deep or troubled waters.
Symbolizes safe passage over the "sea of death".
Represents swift movement and intelligence.
Reminds you of your already considerable knowledge of the deep.
Symbolizes *one who guides*.
One of the Rescue Stones.
A good Dream Stone.
Excellent shield against nightmares.
Outstanding protection stone for infants and children.
Helps prevent emotional breakdowns.
Assists in resolving issues related to mother.
Reminds you to love, accept, and nurture yourself as well as others.
Assists in working with most emotional traumas, including abuse.
Promotes feelings of security and acceptance of who you are.
Stimulates creativity and the desire for freedom.
Helps you deal with internal stresses of all kinds.
A good guide when in "troubled waters".
Protects the defenseless, sensitive, insecure, and vulnerable.
Good reminder to nurture and let yourself be nurtured in return.
Reminds you that play is every bit as important as work.
Assists in problems of, or fears about, being a mother or
       allowing yourself to show the qualities of mothering.

## DOUBLE TERMINATED CRYSTAL

A Double Terminated Crystal is any crystal with a point (termination) at each end. While many crystals are cut and polished to create double terminations, here we will be talking about quartz crystals with natural double terminations. Whether or not a cut and polished Double Terminated Crystal will have the same energy capabilities will depend entirely upon the stone itself, the knowledge and care of the person who shaped it, and, of course, the knowledge and care of the person who uses it.

Naturally Double Terminated Crystals did not grow up with their roots firmly planted in the group matrix, their family, like their brothers and sisters; they are each distinct individuals growing on their own in their own way, with very little or no support from the others around them. These little power houses are very good at reminding you that you have the same qualities within you.

Double Terminated Crystals can take energy in at one point, transform it while holding it, and then shoot it out through the other termination. This is an excellent choice for balancing energies since it encourages a free flow of the energies moving through it. But remember to check the energy flow in your crystal to be sure it moves back and forth from point to point rather than in other ways (see page 5). Not all Double Terminated Crystals have this precise back and forth energy movement, and some even have purely circular energy patterns.

Double Terminated Crystals are good choices for people who need to become an autonomous human being, an essential requirement in your spiritual growth. They are first rate choices for directing and moving energy rapidly from one place to another, especially in crystal patterns or layouts and programs.

Double Terminated Crystals are outstanding communication tools and can usually help keep you energized for longer periods of time than single-terminated crystals. They make excellent psychic development exercise tools and are good choices for most telepathic communication experiments.

Double Terminated Crystals are also good at balancing the right and left hemispheres of the brain, and, in general, are superior at both recharging and balancing almost any kind of energy. These are great confidence builders and excellent protection stones. Carry one anytime you need to give yourself a constant pep talk. (See, also, Herkimer Diamond Quartz Crystal, Spiritual Guardian Quartz Crystal, Mythic Quartz Crystal).

DOUBLE TERMINATED CRYSTAL QUICK REFERENCE:

Symbolizes freedom from the group mind.
Symbolizes your ability to become an autonomous, self-contained individual.
A good Dream Stone.
Outstanding energizer—physically, mentally, emotionally, and spiritually.
Excellent choice when you need to maintain balanced attitudes.
Dramatically boosts telepathic communication.
A good divination stone.
Moves energy swiftly and smoothly from one point to another.
Excellent conductor of energy patterns.
Stimulates and boosts psychic awareness and energy.
Excellent energy stabilizer.
A good stone for achieving and maintaining spiritual balance.
Aids clearer communication of just about anything.
Best choice for directing any type of energy from one place to another.
Helps balance the right and left hemispheres of the brain.
Almost an essential in crystal layout patterns.
Excellent tool when working with your psychic development training.
One of the best choices for anyone who wants to be more comfortable
    with lessons concerning personal freedom.

## DRUSY QUARTZ CRYSTAL

In the mineral world a *druse* is any irregular cavity or opening in a rock or mineral vein whose inner surfaces have become encrusted with minute projecting (often rounded) crystals. The druse is frequently the same mineral as the one surrounding or enclosing it. But all druses are not quartz crystal. A druse forms on many minerals, all of which are called *drusy*. So if you are looking for Drusy Quartz Crystal, ask for it by brand name.

Drusy Quartz Crystal looks very much as if it has been dusted with very small, super-fine crystals forming a thin, crust-like layer over the original matrix or mineral. Drusy Quartz is not the same as a Geode, Crystal Cluster, or Scrubber Crystal (see Crystal Cluster, Geode, Scrubber Crystal). The crystals on these formations will be much larger and more clearly defined. Drusy Quartz can be used in much the same way you would use a Geode, Quartz Cluster or Scrubber Crystal, however; its overall effects will just be much softer and gentler.

This is a good stone to use when you are just beginning something new, when you want to take safe, baby steps toward a goal. Drusy Quartz is one of the best tools when working through any form of self-exploration. With gentleness and sensitivity, this stone helps you find your footing and keep your balance as you inch forward movement-by-movement. Drusy is never harsh or pushy and helps you take things as they come, one experience at a time. It will even wait for you to digest your experiences before helping you to the next one. Drusy Quartz is also a very good choice for anyone who needs to soften or tone down excessive warrior or an overdose of Yang assertive energies.

Drusy Quartz is a good reminder that in matters of the spirit, we are always at a beginning, and that the eventual outcome of even a small step is assured. A Drusy is a good example of patience and trust in your natural growth processes, a reminder to let the rose unfold naturally on its own, to stop trying to push the river.

A good Dream Stone, Drusy Quartz facilitates restful sleep and peaceful dreams. This one is an especially good choice for children of all ages and anyone who is trying to re-establish a child-like wonder of life.

## DRUSY QUARTZ CRYSTAL QUICK REFERENCE:

Symbolizes the beginning of awakening and growth.
Reminds you that you must always begin at the beginning.
Excellent choice for anyone just beginning with crystals.
First rate Dream Stone.
Reminds you to let the rose unfold naturally and on its own.
Calms and soothes what's wrong.
A good, but gentle energizer.
Excellent meditation tool.
Helps connect you with your emotions, safely and sensitively.

DRUSY QUARTZ CRYSTAL continued:

A good manifestation stone, reminding you that most things start small.
Helps soothe all agitated chakra centers.
Reminds you to have patience and trust in your own process.
Good choice for those who often tend to feel small, unimportant, or alone.
Helps you keep your balance while learning to move forward carefully.
Good substitute for a Scrubber Crystal.
Helps you assimilate one experience at a time.
Good tool when working with lessons of patience.
Puts you back in touch with your natural sensitivity.
Good reminder to stop pushing the river.
Excellent choice when beginning new projects of any kind.
Highly recommended when doing any self-exploration.
Automatically turns down the volume of excess assertiveness.
Reminds you that in matters of the spirit, we are all at a beginning.
Excellent for re-establishing your sense of childlike wonder.

EARTHKEEPER CRYSTAL

Earthkeeper Crystals are crystals buried deep in the Earth's crust and can weigh from several hundred pounds to several tons. They are frequently a single crystal rather than a cluster, and often snowy or milky rather than clear. So far the largest single crystal found was in the former USSR and is as tall as a three-story building. Not surprisingly, Earthkeepers are the giants of the Crystal Clan, holding and keeping track of Time and the tiny humans held within Time.

All Earthkeepers emanate a sound frequency at a rate and tone specifically directed at maintaining the energy levels in the locations where they are resting, frequencies appropriate to that specific area of our planet. Earthkeepers help Earth maintain her proper alignment within our universe and in general should probably be left where they're found.

Since most of us will never own an Earthkeeper unless we own the land where one is located, we have to go them, they don't often come to us. Earthkeepers are awesome generators of energy, and if you have never had any side effect symptoms before, hanging around one of these guardians is sure to give you that experience (see page 10).

Earthkeepers can be any type of quartz crystal and in any crystal personality form. Most of them have not yet been located by human beings, and are not likely to be since in most cases their function is uniquely suited to where they rest.

EARTHKEEPER QUICK REFERENCE:

Guardian and protector of the Earth and all of her life forms.
Creates places of power.
Transmits a specific frequency for a specific purpose.

## 8-FACETED CRYSTAL

Any crystal with eight faces (facets) rather than the more usual six is an 8-Faceted Crystal. These crystals are rare since quartz crystals always try to grow six sides.

8-Faceted Crystals have the extra-special ability to activate energy around them in tune with all of the frequencies governed by the symbolism and sound of the number 8. Symbolically the number 8 is the number for Infinity and Cosmic Consciousness. It is also the number of regeneration; renewal after an initiation; abundance; the reality of the physical world; perfect balance and rhythm; the goal of the spiritual Initiate; entrance into a new state or condition of the Soul; and all possibilities contained within manifestation. Eight is the number assigned to Hermes and Thoth and the equivalent of the Hebrew IHVH. To the ancient Hindu 8 X 8 was the number of the Celestial World as it is established on Earth.

This Crystal is associated with prosperity, success, and accomplishment, making it an excellent stone to have around when pursuing a business venture or planning a career, and to remind you that your possibilities are indeed endless. Paired with an Abundance Crystal, a good attitude and some effort on your part, it would be hard to miss your target.

An 8-Faceted Crystal helps you learn to balance your desire for material things with your spiritual growth. It is an excellent reminder that it is entirely possible to be wealthy and spiritual at the same time, and that you are never stuck with the common, ordinary pattern of life or growth that everyone expects of you.

An 8-Faceted Crystal is an excellent tool for recharging the human aura and maintaining your spiritual equilibrium. It is a first rate communication tool, especially for communicating with your guides, teachers, and Higher or Inner Self.

## 8-FACETED CRYSTAL QUICK REFERENCE:

Symbolizes Infinity, Perfection, and the Initiate.
Symbolizes Cosmic Consciousness.
Represents regeneration and renewal at the physical level.
Outstanding for balancing the power of Spirit with the power of Nature.
Represents success, accomplishment, growth, and abundance.
Excellent tool for aiding you to enter into a new state of being.
Represents the spiraling movement of the Universe.
A superb Dream Stone.
Very specialized energy activator.
Helps balance your material desires with spiritual ones.
Reminds you that you are not trapped by the forms of your culture.
One of the best protection stones.
Balances Yang (male) energy.

8-FACETED CRYSTAL continued:

Excellent choice to focus your concentration.
Aids in releasing fear of your personal power and how you will use it.
Superior divination tool.
Assists in communication with your Higher Self.
Helps you deal with fear of your physical death.
Great tool for balancing your emotions.
Reminds you that it's okay to be wealthy and spiritual at the same time.
Recharges and revitalizes the human aura.
Reminds you of your true position within the physical world.
A symbol of regeneration and renewal.
Represents all of the possibilities within the physical world.
Helps you balance your desire for the material with the spiritual.
Good reminder that you don't have to be what others see.
Symbolizes entrance into a new state of being.

ELESTIAL CRYSTAL

Elestial Crystals are unlike any other known form of quartz crystal. Sometimes called Skeleton Quartz, many of them appear to have been singed by fire and have a smoky, even burned, look. This is the youngest form of quartz crystal on our planet, but since most quartz is somewhere between 100 to 125 million years old this doesn't mean much in human terms.

Elestials also often resemble the human brain and for this reason symbolize the higher qualities of the mind. Elestials don't generally have sharp points; many of their terminations will be tabular, rectangular, or square, the corners slightly rounded rather than pointed. The easiest thing to say about how an Elestial looks is that it is just plain "other-than" and does not in the slightest resemble any other form of quartz crystal. Run to your nearest mineral store and ask to see one and you'll know exactly what we mean.

Almost all Elestials have odd cryptic markings on their surfaces or deep within the crystal itself. These can sometimes even have the appearance of esoteric hieroglyphics. Some authorities believe that these markings are a type of cosmic alphabet, carrying information of Universal laws not originally of Earth-origin.

Elestials are also said to carry pre-physical non-terrestrial information, allowing you to access information related to why you chose the life you are now living on planet Earth. Elestials can also assist you in coming to terms with being in the Third Dimension, and in coming to terms with leaving it when that time comes.

Elestial Crystals are exceptional tools to assist you in dissolving deep emotional bonds unconsciously formed during early infancy and childhood. Elestials help you to travel through non-time-related dimensions, bring that

43

information back with you into this timeframe, and then help you put it together to get a better understanding of "the big picture" and your part in it, especially when used with a piece of Fluorite (Fluorite keeps things practical).

ELESTIAL CRYSTAL QUICK REFERENCE:

Symbolizes ancient Universal laws.
Symbolizes the Higher Human Mind.
One of the Power Stones.
A great tool when working with old karmic emotional bonds.
Assists in avoiding mental and emotional breakdowns.
Contains pre-physical information.
Helps you work with unremembered childhood issues.
A good tool to use for getting the "Big Picture".
Aids in travel through dimensions which are not limited by Time.
Good tool for releasing the physical at the times it is most appropriate.
Assists in dissolving or working with unproductive emotional attachments.
Alleviates fear of this dimension and of being involved with physical matter.
Great tool for remembering why you chose this particular Earth life.
Helps you access and bring back other-dimensional information.
Believed to carry encoded information concerning Universal laws.
Reminds you that even the most ordered life forms do not always
        outwardly appear as you think they should.

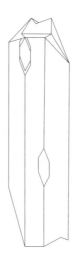

## EMPATHIC CRYSTAL

Empathic Crystals are quartz crystals which have been mishandled and badly treated at sometime in their lives. Their points (terminations) are often severely damaged or missing altogether. Through no fault of their own, these are considered the unattractive and therefore ignored, unappreciated members of the Crystal Clan. Empaths have been dropped, smacked with chisels and hammers, tossed carelessly in a box and put on a dusty back shelf, and just simply undervalued.

Empathic Crystals are the specialists at empathizing with you on days when you feel unloved, unappreciated, or just plain unattractive and unlovable. These crystals are also specialists at helping you open your heart, and of protecting the already open-hearted from absorbing too much of the pain of others.

Empaths are the experts at reminding you that you can have compassion for others without shredding yourself in the process. If you are feeling swamped or drained by someone else's pain, hold an Empath and let it absorb what you feel. Now bury it in sea or rock salt crystals or let it rest on a bed of sage and copper until you intuitively know when it is ready to face the world again. And then say, "Thank you", loud and clear. (For more on cleansing crystals see page 8).

As many Empathic Crystals sooner or later develop spectacular internal rainbows, they are excellent reminders that it is who you are on the inside that matters, and that it is possible to generate your own rainbows even when you have been badly treated, neglected, pushed around, ignored, and even dropped on your head and heart a few times. And given the overall symbolism of quartz crystal, an Empath is a perfect symbol for the smaller self who is willing to sacrifice itself to the Greater Self.

Empaths are outstanding teddy bear stones to tell your troubles. They always, always listen and understand on some level. And sometimes they even begin to help you change the things around you. Having been where you are, they know how it feels and what to do about it. They, of course, make great Dream Stones.

EMPATHIC CRYSTAL QUICK REFERENCE:

Symbolizes the smaller self willingly in submission to the Greater Self.
Represents your ability to conquer all adversity.
One of the best Rescue Stones around.
Excellent Dream Stone.
Outstanding as a "teddy bear" stone.
Helps alleviate feelings of loss, fear, and grief.
A good tool to use when working with addictions of any kind.
Helps release anxieties and fear of being unlovable.
Good divination stone.
Balances both Yin (female) and Yang (male) energies.
An excellent tool for working with all ego-related lessons.
Helps you work with depression.
Excellent choice during times of change and transition.
Highly recommended for anyone who has been abused in any way at any time.
Helps you become more open to others, but a reminder to not take on
their pain if you really want to help them.
Reminds you it's who you are and what you can do that matters,
not how you look or what others think about how you look.

ET CRYSTAL

An ET Crystal is a crystal that has one point or termination on one end and several terminations on the other, causing it to look very much like an old fashioned science fiction rocketship.

These crystals have the power to bring energy in at their single point and transmit it out through each of the terminations at the other end—in other words they are capable of "spraying" energy (a good way to spark up any room). And of course the reverse is also true; ET Crystals can take in immense quantities of energy at their multiple terminations and then focus it in laser-like fashion through their single termination.

ETs are also good choices for people who are interested in the life and times outside this planet's atmosphere. ETs are good reminders that life comes in many sizes, shapes, colors, and even dimensions. These are also good reminders that the human species isn't the only advanced form of life in our universe and are good choices for pairing with Elestials (not to mention Moldavite and Selenite).

ET Crystals are first rate gifts for people who need their own unique brand of creativity boosted and brought forward into their daily lives. This is an especially good choice for scientists, artists, musicians, teachers, and all space travellers.

Since many ETs were also once Self Healed Crystals, they are exceptional energy rechargers and personal motivators; a good choice for entrepreneurs of all kinds.

ET CRYSTAL QUICK REFERENCE:

Symbolizes your connection to the Universe.
Great tool for communication with off-world life.
Has the ability to function as a laser for intense focusing of energy.
Can be used to collect and then "spray" energy.
A superior energy recharger.
Helps you build and maintain self-confidence.
A good channelling tool.
Stimulates feelings of courage.
Excellent energy shield.
Helps you deal with fears of all kinds.
Reminds you that we all are many individuals within the One.
Acts as a collector of energy through its multi-terminations.
Reminds you that you not only can heal yourself but can go beyond
         to an entirely new form of being and power.

GENERATOR CRYSTAL

Generator Crystals are crystals terminating in six faces (facets), all coming to a near-perfect point at the top-center of the crystal. Generators are sometimes also called Projector Crystals. A Generator Crystal can be found as small as 1/4 inch or be as large as a tall building. These are always powerful stones, no matter what their size, and should be treated with care and much respect.

Generators do exactly what their name implies—they generate and project energy. These are first rate group meditation tools when seated in the center of a meditation circle. Generators are also outstanding at re-energizing or recharging other crystals and stones.

These crystals are often favorites of those involved in alternative healing procedures, generating and directing energy in extremely precise regular pulses and patterns, especially when programmed for specific functions.

Some Generators have been known to generate enough energy to crack and shatter other crystals in their near vicinity, so be careful where you place them and how you use them. But if you have any doubts that all this crystal energy stuff really works, experiment with your Generator. Just be prepared for what you experience—and remember that it is not nice to point.

Like all stones, each Generator is a distinct individual with its own lifetime of experiences and unique frequency transmissions. It can be cloudy at the base and clear at its point, or vice versa; it can contain phantoms, rainbows, inclusions; and it can be perfectly clear. A Generator can be any member of the Quartz Clan so long as all of its six sides terminate in one regular 6-sided point. Generators, however, do not have to be "perfect" to function.

Generators also symbolize the number 6. Six, among many other interpretations, is the number of accomplishment, purpose, and growth. It symbolizes the completion of a process and often shows up in your life at the end of a period of great change and activity. It is your experiences with the number 6 which prepares you for the lessons of the number 7. Six is also the number of the Philosopher's Stone, The Shield of David, the Seal of Solomon with the power to bind negative energies, and 6 can symbolize sexuality since it represents the hexagram which itself denotes the meeting of male and female. Six was a perfect number to Pythagoras since it was the midpoint between the 2 of the beginning of growth and the 10 of completion.

Generators are extraordinary meditation tools, helping you gather and focus your concentration and energy, then amplify and send it anywhere you like. They are also good instructors while you are learning not to damage anything when focusing and using energy and power responsibly. Wear or carry a Generator anytime you need to feel strong and in control. Generators are perfect mates for Receiver Crystals.

## GENERATOR CRYSTAL QUICK REFERENCE:

Symbolizes the union of Fire and Water which when harmoniously
        combined creates the Human Soul.
Represents the number 6 with all of its symbolism.
One of the best Power Stones, directly symbolizing the power use energy.
A Shaman Stones.
Outstanding for generating, concentrating, and projecting energy.
Good reminder when you are serious about accomplishing anything.
Superb tool for focusing and storing energy.
A good choice for leaders of any kind.
Helps recharge all energy systems.
Generates strong feelings of self-confidence and personal courage.
First rate meditation tool.
Breaks up and dissolves feelings of apathy and lethargy.
Outstanding channelling tool.
Good choice during any rebirthing procedures.
Matchless physical and psychic protection tool.
Great aid in dealing with a fear of heights or flying.
A good tool for digging for your core beliefs.
Connects you more directly to your Higher and Inner Self.
Outstanding choice for business people.
Balances energy directly and quickly.
One of the best telepathic communication tools.
Helps generate and maintain your energy during spiritual exercises.
Excellent candidate for programming.

# GEODE

Geodes are a form of Crystal Cluster, usually surrounded by another type of quartz (like Agate). Geodes are small closed crystal systems, as opposed to large caves, although technically all crystal caves are simply very large Geodes extending for miles rather than inches or feet.

Geodes contain the properties of quartz crystal and their surrounding mineral. For example, a Geode with an Agate outer shell has all of the general qualities of both Quartz Crystal Clusters (including the particular variety of quartz crystal, e.g., Smoky Quartz, Amethyst) and the variety and color of Agate surrounding the crystals inside the Geode. Quite a power combination, to say the least.

For instance, all Agates carry ancient legends of being used to boost the immune system, stimulate more tolerant attitudes, for helping us stay grounded during highly emotional situations, balance and energize all of the chakras, relieve muscle tension...and on and on and on. In short, there isn't much that almost any variety of Agate hasn't been used by our ancestors.

Geodes are an excellent choice for any environment in dire need of harmony, serenity, protection, and a productive stimulating exchange of thought and ideas. They are superb choices for conference or meeting rooms, especially the large Amethyst Geodes (often called Amethyst Cathedrals).

Geodes are known to contain information for a specific person, very much like a Record Keeper Crystal. The person who is ready to retrieve the Geode's information will automatically be attracted to the right Geode at the right time.

Examine the crystals growing within the shelter of your Geode carefully. As with all Crystal Clusters, they will probably contain many crystal forms within one Geode. These are perfect companions for Devic Crystals, and if you want to improve communication even more, try adding a pieced of Pyrite.

## GEODE QUICK REFERENCE:

Symbolizes shelter and protection while growing.
Represents your ability to function harmoniously as an individual in a group.
Symbolizes the Microcosm of the Macrocosm.
A Crystal Cave and an outstanding meditation tool.
First rate protection stone.
Stimulates and maintains creative levels of energy.
Recommended for meeting rooms of all kinds.
Stimulates a strong desire for compatibility and cooperation.
Connects directly to Nature energies.
Excellent choice for children.
Stimulates clear thinking and creative ideas.
Often contains specific information for a particular person or persons.
Promotes and generates a desire for cooperation and harmony.
Reminds us that we are all part of a larger family or group.
Carries all the symbolism of a Crystal Cluster and its surrounding mineral.

51

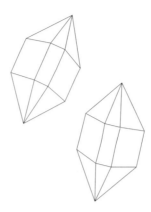

## HERKIMER DIAMOND CRYSTAL

Herkimer Diamond Crystals are small, exceptionally clear, double terminated quartz crystals, and always barrel-shaped. Unlike other crystals, Herkimers do not generally have to be chemically cleaned before marketing; they just naturally shine like Diamonds. Although there are now Herkimer look-alikes on the market, true Herkimers are found only in Herkimer County, New York and are becoming almost impossible to find in the commercial market-place. Consequently, this is another crystal to be sure to ask for by brand name.

True Herkimers are the power horse of the Crystal Clan, no matter what their size. The size of any Herkimer has little, if any, impact on its energy and power. Herkimers are excellent for generating and maintaining smooth and balanced energy flow wherever you need it, anytime you need it.

These are the non-conformists of the Crystal Clan. Herkimers have the courage to be born differently and alone, without the support of others, and to continue to stand alone and shine, no matter what, even after removal from their original supportive environment. These tiny crystals lend this same strength and energy to their human companions. Herkimers help you get in touch with your own brand of individuality, reminding you that only when standing alone with no apparent visible support to stabilize you are you able to tap into your inner strength and wisdom, that ultimately you must learn to trust and lean on nothing outside of your true Self.

Herkimers are extraordinary at helping you maintain a more balanced personality. These tiny little guys just naturally stimulate your creativity and intuition, amplifying and maximizing your natural talents. They are outstanding at stimulating and boosting your natural clairvoyant and psychic capacities and in helping you access and work with past life or parallel life memories. Herkimers also maximize your memory retention, especially when worn or used with Rhodochrosite.

Herkimers are truly superb at balancing all types of energy. Wearing or carrying Herkimers when you are going through bad physical or emotional cycles can help you keep your equilibrium, as nearly effortlessly and painlessly as possible.

In spite of their small size, all Herkimers are able to store enormous quantities of information, making them outstanding choices for programming and crystal layout patterns. Herkimers are also excellent sleep and Dream Stones, actively stimulating clear visions and dreams. And, of course, they are good choices for any and all meditation and concentration exercises.

Primary cleansers of the emotional, mental, and physical energy bodies, Herkimers can help you raise your energy level, clear it, and remember where you were when you left that level after entering other levels.

In short, there aren't many things Herkimers can't do for you. Think POWER and ENERGY when you think of Herkimers.

HERKIMER DIAMOND QUICK REFERENCE:

Symbolizes your ability to be a powerful individual completely on your own.
The power horse of the Crystal Clan.
One of the major Power Stones.
A good Rescue Stone.
Outstanding Dream Stone.
One of the Shaman Stones.
Allows uncluttered telepathic communication.
Maximizes your natural psychic abilities and awareness.
Harmonizes all chakras at all levels.
Cleanses all of the subtle energy bodies.
Maximizes your natural intuitive capacities.
An excellent choice to achieve and maintain balance of any and all kinds.
Increases your memory capacity and retention.
Helps access past or parallel life memories.
Helps you maintain vast amounts of spiritual energy.
Generates immense amounts of physical energy.
Helps maintain smooth and balanced energy flows at all levels.
Stimulates the courage to be and remain an autonomous individual.
Helps you *know* you can do it, not just hope you can.
Keeps you strongly aligned to your true essence.
Reminds you to act from inner integrity, always.
Stimulates a strong desire for personal freedom and independence.
Outstanding choice for business people.
Reminds you who you are and to act always from that inner knowledge.
A good tool for communicating with your teachers and guides.
Reminds you that ultimately you must learn to lean on nothing
        outside your true Self.

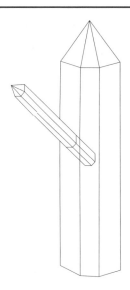

INNER CHILD CRYSTAL

An Inner Child Crystal is one or more crystals *partially* embedded in another crystal. These crystals very much resemble a parent holding, cradling, and in some cases giving birth to, a child, represented by the smaller crystal. An Inner Child can also be a smaller crystal cradled between two parent crystals. An Inner Child Crystal is not the same as a Creator Crystal or a Phantom (see Creator Crystal and Phantom Crystal).

Symbolically, the Inner Child Crystal and the parent holding it represent the dependance of one upon the other. If the larger parent crystal does not hold or support the smaller, the parent will soon be left with an empty place where the child rested, while the smaller crystal will be left with no shelter or support before it has fully matured.

An Inner Child Crystal makes a great friend when you are feeling particularly insecure or off-balance. This is an excellent stone for anyone needing to be held and cared for—physically, emotionally, psychologically, or spiritually.

An Inner Child is a good protection stone for the child in you and a reminder to keep in touch with the child-like parts of your nature, like trust and having fun with simple everyday things. An Inner Child Crystal helps remind you to respect the needs and feelings of the small child you never leave behind, and that it is okay to be "spiritual" and still have fun, even silly slapstick fun. It reminds you that play is as essential to your overall growth and development as work and study.

An Inner Child Crystal is also a good choice for helping you get back in touch with your prime directives, what you came here to learn, and is a good tool to help you remember and work with any uncompleted childhood lessons or buried memories (you might want to pair it with an Elestial for this kind of work). It is, of course, outstanding for any inner child work.

INNER CHILD CRYSTAL QUICK REFERENCE:

Symbolizes the deep relatedness between parent and child.
Represents the inner child in each of us.
One of the best Rescue Stones.
A good Dream Stone.
Outstanding choice during any inner child work.
Excellent emotional and physical protection stone.
A good reminder that we each still carry our childhood with us.
Helps you release and safely discharge internal stresses.
Great aid in relieving sadness and depression.
Reminds you that you are never, ever totally alone or without support.
Assists in any problems you have with being a parent.
Promotes love and acceptance of yourself.
A good meditation stone.
Helps prevent emotional breakdowns.
Great tool when learning to regain your child-like trust of life.
Reminds you to be supportive of others.
An excellent choice when entering new territories that kick up old fears.
Reminds us to have fun and be child-like, but not child-ish.
Recommended for anyone fighting any type of addiction.
Helps with emotional traumas connected to being or having been a human child.
Reminds you that fun and play are as essential for your spiritual growth
as work and study.

ISIS CRYSTAL

An Isis Crystal is any crystal with at least one 5-sided face, often shaped like the one above. The number 5 itself symbolizes The Center, love, health, knowledge, Essence acting upon Matter, the Human Soul, rapid change, and things not yet complete. Five is also symbolic of the harmonious union of Yin and Yang, meditation, marriage, religion, and the potential for liberation from the mundane or material.

So an Isis Crystal can remind you of all of these things, and that the human soul is always moving toward re-union with its Source, even though it may still be seeing itself as incomplete and imperfect.

An Isis Crystal connects you more directly to the higher side of your Yin (female) characteristics and nature, whether you are male or female, and amplifies all of the more positive qualities of Yin while controlling or suppressing all of the less productive ones. Using an Isis Crystal during meditation can help you access lost or scattered memories of times you utilized the Yin side of your energy for the benefit of others, and this applies to men as well as women.

Isis is *She Who Brings Forth* and symbolizes fidelity in love, perseverance under seemingly impossible conditions, courage, compassion, humility, acceptance, wisdom, fertility, and magnanimousness towards all living things. An Egyptian religious text dated approximately 3,000 B.C. states, "In the beginning there was Isis, Oldest of the Old." She was "the One Who Is All"," the Lady of the Red Apparel", "the Bearer of Wings, Source of the Gods and Giver of Life". It was Isis who revealed the secrets of the stars to humanity and held dominion over all words of power. To be initiated into the mysteries of Isis was to automatically obtain a privileged status in the Afterlife. Isis was linked to the Sirius Star System by her followers and Osiris to the Orion system (see Osiris Crystal).

An Isis Crystal is an especially good choice as a Dream Stone when working with issues related to the symbolism of Isis or the number 5, and of course is the perfect mate for an Osiris Crystal.

ISIS CRYSTAL QUICK REFERENCE:

Symbolizes the human soul in its search for completion.
Represents Words of Power.
Symbolizes human destiny.
Represents Wisdom, Justice, and fidelity in love.
Symbolizes courage in the face of great adversity.
A good Dream Stone.
One of the Rescue Stones.
A Shaman Stone.
Attracts and then helps you hold on to human love.
Amplifies the higher side of your Yin (female) qualities.
Helps you put your ego in proper perspective.
A great aid when coping with grief and issues of loss.
Helps you work with fear of life itself.
Enhances your compatibility with all types of people.
Helps you regain any lost Yin qualities and wisdom.
One of the fertility stones.
Helps teach patience and perseverance against seemingly impossible odds.
Stimulates a desire for faithfulness in love.
Traditionally, believed to help benefit the female reproductive system.
Represents beauty, courage, and patience in the face of great odds.
Controls and suppresses the less desirable qualities of Yin.
Represents the Divine Mother, the Queen of Heaven, She Who Brings Forth
the Sun, Source of the Gods, the One Who Is All.

## LASER WAND CRYSTAL

Lasers are long, thin crystals resembling a wand. They can be anywhere from 1/4 inch to several inches in length but will always have either sharp 3-sided points [terminations] or a slightly rounded point often resembling a human finger. Either form is a Laser Wand Crystal. Lasers are not Generator or Artemis Crystals, they are their own highly specialized form (see Generator Crystal, Artemis Crystal). Few, if any, Lasers will be perfectly clear and they often look slightly secondhand or battered. A Laser Wand Crystal is also sometimes called a Merlin Crystal.

Laser Wands are often used by those involved in alternative healing procedures to direct the flow of energy in a very precise surgical-like manner through the Laser into the organ or area being treated. Lasers can be used very much like a non-cutting scalpel by trained healers, but are used only to work with energy frequency patterns, never to actually cut or damage the skin.

Laser Wand Crystals don't need to be confined to use by alternative healers and they make excellent "magic wands". Lasers are outstanding candidates for programming and to help you focus energy toward accomplishing your goals. Properly programmed, Laser Wands are first rate protection stones. They are also good substitutes for an Artemis Crystal, usually a much harder crystal to find. But again, remember that it isn't nice to point.

LASER WAND CRYSTAL QUICK REFERENCE:

Symbolizes focus and your determination to reach your goals.
The Merlin Crystal.
One of the Power Stones.
One of the Shaman Stones.
A good Rescue Stone.
Focuses and directs energy with precision and accuracy.
Helps you fight and overcome unreasonable fears.
Excellent telepathic communication tool.
A good physical and psychic protection stone.
Fine re-energizer.
Good choice for communication with your Higher Self.
Promotes a more self-confident attitude.
Good choice for programming.
Often used by those working with energy in alternative healing fields.
A good "magic wand" to help you focus your thoughts and desires.

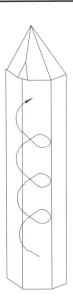

LEFT HANDED CRYSTAL

A quartz crystal with an extra face (facet) on the left side of the larger face of the crystal is called a Left Handed Crystal. This simply means that the crystal spiral within the crystal itself flows naturally to the left, and even the experts don't agree why. This spiral usually cannot be seen with the naked eye (see page 2).

Left Handed Crystals are just naturally more receptive at drawing in energy when held in the left hand or placed on the left side of the body, and especially so if they are also Receiver Crystals. Left Handed Crystals also have the ability to draw out unwanted, undesirable, unproductive energy patterns. These crystals help activate the right side of the human brain and integrate right brain functions with those of the left.

Left Handed Crystals are recommended for anyone wishing to boost their natural intuitive talents, psychic awareness, access to personal spiritual insights, and any right brain functions, including creativity.

This one is a good balance for a Right Handed Crystal, a Generator Crystal, Generator-Receiver, or a Laser Wand Crystal, and for harmonizing excessive Yang (male) energies.

As a symbol, the Left is an ancient one for the external, passive, in-coming energy of the Soul. Some authorities also view left as the past, and right as the present or future.

## LEFT HANDED CRYSTAL QUICK REFERENCE:

Symbolizes the incoming energy of the Soul.
Represents all right brain functions.
Symbolizes Yin (female) energies.
Excellent Dream Stone.
Stimulates and boosts your natural creativity.
Helps activate and integrate all right brain functions.
Encourages patience, tolerance, and compassion.
A good telepathic communication tool.
Helps balance or harmonize any excessive Yang (male) energies.
A good balance for Right Handed, Generator, Generator-Receiver,
        and Laser Wand Crystals.
Can be used to slow down or speed up the activities of the
        right brain hemisphere.

LEVEL QUARTZ CRYSTAL

Level Quartz is a quartz crystal which managed to trap an ancient drop of water while the crystal was still forming. This trapped water can be seen when you look into the crystal, and often moves back and forth like the bubble in a carpenter's level. Level Quartz is reasonably rare and should never be left in direct sunlight. This ancient water will evaporate and might not recondense.

Use Level Quartz Crystals to test your balance and to help you regain any lost balance or equilibrium. This is an outstanding communication device, assisting communication on all levels of energy through the medium of both the crystal and water, and all that they each symbolize.

As containers of an ancient element (water), Level Quartz Crystals can help you access physical time: past, present, and future. Water itself is an extremely complex symbol with one of the widest ranges of interpretation. In many cultures, water is seen as the creator and the primal origin of all life. Water is the source of all potentials within physical existence and often symbolizes the Unmanifest, the Great Mother, and the Yin (feminine) principle. Water also represents the continuity and yet constant changes inherent within all physical life forms. In the form of Level Quartz, water is surrounded and formed by quartz crystal—WOW!

LEVEL QUARTZ CRYSTAL QUICK REFERENCE:

Symbolizes perfect balance attainable within the material world.
Represents Spirit contained, held, and shaped within Matter.
Exceptional Dream Stone.
A great aid in checking and maintaining energy balances of any kind.
Allows you access to the concepts of physical Time.
Outstanding communication tool.
Useful tool for those afraid of heights.
Excellent tool for accessing Earth history and information.
Recommended for anyone unnaturally fearful of being here on Earth.
Reminds you of your enormous potential within the physical.

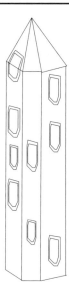

LIBRARY CRYSTAL

Library Crystals are crystals with several, newer, flat, stubby crystals plastered to the outside surface of the larger crystal. These overlays are not well-defined crystals but literally overgrowths and often resemble a layer of thick plaster or paste. Unlike an Abundance or Comet Crystal, overgrowth crystals on the surface of a Library will never have the typical crystalline shape.

Depending upon the stone, a Library Crystal carries either several pages or several volumes of information encoded within these overgrowth crystals on its surface, in addition to the information held within the main body deep within the Library. As you may have guessed, Libraries are the kissing cousins of Record Keeper Crystals.

Library Crystals are generally just that—they hold information accessible by the general public and not necessarily for specific individuals. You do, however, have to be ready to put some effort into accessing and referencing the information in your Library, just as you do in any library. And don't forget to take notes while you're in there. And you do get to ask for help in your research from the Head Librarian.

LIBRARY CRYSTAL QUICK REFERENCE:

Symbolizes stored information and knowledge from many cultures and times.
Good choice for anyone who wishes to begin any course of study.
Outstanding Dream Stone.
Exceptional meditation tool.

LIBRARY CRYSTAL continued:

Stores ancient and multi-dimensional information.
A good confidence builder.
Effective tool for working with ego-related lessons.
Helps you access and work with your personal belief systems.
Excellent divination tool.
Helps in accessing past, present, and future information.
A good tool when communicating with your teachers and guides.
Good choice for working with fear of your personal power.
Great general crystal research tool.
A reminder that Eternity is a very long time indeed.

## LIFE PATH CRYSTAL

Life Path Crystals are long, thin crystals with one or more *totally smooth* sides. Run your finger up and down the sides of your crystal. If you find absolutely no imperfections of any kind, you have been fortunate enough to find your Life Path Crystal—no small achievement. Life Path Crystals are sometimes also called Beauty Way Crystals.

Life Path Crystals are good meditation and spiritual exercise tools and can be used to help you find and stay on your path. Focusing on this crystal can also help pull you back onto your path and be a constant reminder that your intention is to accomplish certain things within this lifetime.

For instance, one way to use your Life Path Crystal is to hold it in your hands and repeat your daily affirmations or goals into it each morning. Use any words or phrases that have strong personal impact. They do not have to be lofty or "spiritual" to work—they just have to have deep, intense, personal meaning. Then check in again with your Life Path at the end of your day to see how it feels about how you carried out your intentions.

A Life Path Crystal can help you learn to flow with the current of your life and encourage you to open to your natural inner rhythms. A Life Path can help connect you more directly to your Higher and Inner Self to ensure that you accomplish what you originally set out to do, and at the same time keep you on track with your original pre-physical plan or blueprint.

These crystals are excellent at reminding you of what is truly important in your life and growth, helping you naturally and effortlessly shed what is unnecessary or stopping the natural flow. A Life Path Crystal is one of the best choices for directing you towards the answers to "Who am I?" and "Why am I here?", especially when paired with a piece of Sugilite.

## LIFE PATH CRYSTAL QUICK REFERENCE:

Symbolizes your path in this life.
One of the Shaman Stones.
Excellent Dream Stone.
A good Rescue Stone.
Helps you remember to go with the flow.
An excellent protection stone.
Helps you remember your present life path.
Connects you more directly to your Higher and Inner Self.
Exceptional meditation stone.
Helps you generate the courage to stay on your true path.
One of the best affirmation tools around.
Good divination stone.
Generates psychic intuitive energy.
Excellent tool for accessing your belief systems.
First rate energy shield.
A good depression fighter.

LIFE PATH CRYSTAL continued:

One of the best spiritual balance tools.
Outstanding channelling tool.
Good choice for entrepreneurs of any kind.
Stimulates attitudes of compassion for all forms of life.
Helps build spiritual confidence.
Outstanding telepathic communication tool.
Good choice when making major life decisions.
Constant reminder of what is truly important in your life.
Helps you recognize and discard the unnecessary things in your life.
One of the best for communicating with your teachers and guides.
A good choice for dealing with lessons concerned with loss, grief, and death.
Helps you work with lessons concerning your personal power.
Directs you toward the answers to "Who am I?" and "Why am I here?"

## MASTER CHANNELLING CRYSTAL

A Master Channelling Crystal is any quartz crystal with seven facets (faces) in place of the more common five or six. Since most quartz crystals try to form six facets, a 7-faceted quartz crystal is relatively rare.

Please note that we said seven *facets*, not seven lines defining the facets. A Master Channeller is not the same crystal as a Channelling Crystal (a Channelling Crystal has one 7-sided facet and one 3-sided facet directly opposite it; see Channelling Crystal).

A Master Channeller is often found in the form of Amethyst quartz crystal, creating an exceptionally good tool for connecting to and then receiving information from any higher or faster-moving energy sources.

The seven facets of the Master Channeller symbolize the Mystic Student, the Spiritual Seeker, the one who goes within to find true wisdom. In short, a Master Channelling Crystal is just that—a crystal that helps you receive (channel) information from your teaching masters. In fact, the only equals to a Master Channeller for this function are Kyanite and Selenite.

## MASTER CHANNELLING CRYSTAL QUICK REFERENCE:

Symbolizes the True Spiritual Seeker, the one who goes within to find wisdom.
Represents all interpretations of the number 7.
One of the Rescue Stones.
Exceptional Dream Stone.
One of the best meditation tools around.
Symbolizes the 7 steps necessary for you to reach the seventh spiritual level.
Aids directly in receiving information from your teaching masters.
Reminds you that the seemingly impossible is quite possible after all.

## MASTER MATRIX CRYSTAL

Master Matrix Crystals will have most, if not all, of the currently known geometric shapes etched or engraved *naturally* somewhere on the outside of the crystal or hidden deep within its interior. As you can imagine, these stones are exceptionally rare. A Master Matrix Crystal can be any variety of quartz crystal and any crystal personality, and is sometimes called a Root Directory or Master Programmer Crystal.

A Master Matrix contains all of the hard data necessary to program or reboot Record Keeper Crystals. These are the master programmers, the matrix stones used to program the original Record Keeper Crystals.

Use your Master Matrix in the same way you would use a computer's root directory. This is fairly advanced stuff and not recommended for those without the patience to gain the knowledge and experience to use them responsibly. And just like any sophisticated computer system, improper use could cause the loss of critical data, and give you a screaming headache in the bargain.

You should be aware that you cannot change the original underlying program of any Master Matrix, but you *can* add to them, creating subdirectories to run from the main program. These subdirectories can be used to expand the information already existing in a Record Keeper Crystal as well as increase the crystal's storage capacity for new and additional information. Master Matrix Crystals can also, of course, be used to create your own Record Keeper Crystals.

Master Matrix Crystals are not often immediately recognizable and they certainly are not likely to be beautiful. In fact they are very often quite the reverse. As with other deep knowledge, "the secret protects itself" and is neither easily found nor deciphered, probably one of the reasons why these stones are sometimes not particularly attractive or eye-catching.

Treat this crystal with the greatest respect and honor. To try to misuse it would begin a chain of events you definitely will not want to experience first-hand in this or any other lifetime.

MASTER MATRIX QUICK REFERENCE:

Symbolizes the sum total of all information available to humanity within the present time cycle.
A Master Programmer of all Record Keepers.
An excellent Dream Stone.
Superior channelling stone.
Aids in accessing your belief systems.
Good information source to help you in making the most appropriate decisions.
Allows you to create your own Record Keepers.
Repositories of esoteric knowledge and information.
A good tool for communicating with your guides, teachers, and Higher Self.
Good tool for expanding the information stored in other crystals, especially Record Keeper Crystals.
Excellent choice for working with any fears concerning death and your concept of what happens after physical death.

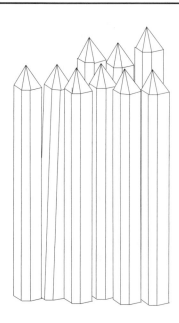

## MUSE CRYSTAL

A Quartz Crystal Cluster of nine crystals of similar size and length symbolizes the Nine Muses, the nine Greek goddesses who preside over the Arts. There must be exactly nine crystals clustered together, no more and no less. Deliberately breaking nine crystals out of a cluster doesn't count, tempting as it is. The formation must be natural and as you can imagine is rare, just making it all the more fun to search for yours. Muse Crystals are also, of course, Triple Quantums (see Quantum Crystal).

Muse Crystals enhance all forms of creative expression. They directly and vigorously stimulate an appreciation for natural beauty in all of its forms: music, art, poetry, literature, dance, and all other expressions of creativity. Art includes creating your own business, creating special environments, designing clothes, cooking, building strong friendships, raising healthy and happy children, and almost anything else human beings do. This is an excellent stone for both highly creative people and anyone who wants to awaken their natural creativity or remind themselves of the creativity inherent in each one of us.

Muses remind you to see the artistic beauty in everything—people's actions, violent storms, and even things you have been avoiding or frightened of up till now. Muses make first rate Dream Stones, surfacing through your dream symbols pertinent information about any creative project or creative decision you are trying to make. They are also excellent divination stones, allowing you a more direct connection to the symbolism of the Muses. A Muse Crystal can, of course, also help you reattach to the creativity involved in your spiritual quest or path.

Symbolically, the Nine Muses represent the sum total of all human learning: Thalia (music); Clio (history); Calliope (heroic poetry); Terpsichore (dance); Melpomene (tragedy); Erato (erotic poetry); Eoterpe (flute accompaniment); Polyhymnia (sacred songs); and Urania (the Celestial Aphrodite of the plane of fixed stars). In ancient legends, it was the Muses who were responsible for inventing the seven-tone musical scale which they based on the Seven Heavenly Spheres. The Nine Muses were originally the Triple Muse and directly associated with the Moon Goddess. It was not until sometime around 2,500 B.C. that the Triple Muse became the Ninefold Goddess, the triple trinity of Creator-Preserver-Destroyer.

MUSE CRYSTAL QUICK REFERENCE:

Symbolizes the Nine Muses, the sum total of human learning.
Represents the Triple Trinity of Creator-Preserver-Destroyer.
Ignites inspiration, the imagination, and exceptionally high levels of creativity.
Awakens your latent creative energies.
First rate Dream Stone.
Outstanding channelling tool.
Superior booster of natural creative energies.
A Triple Quantum Crystal.
One of the best for creativity of all kinds.
Helps you see the artistic and creative aspects of life at all levels.
A good tool for attracting, holding, and focusing creative energies of all kinds.
Especially recommended for anyone involved in or with the Arts.
Generates and helps sustain an appreciation for Nature and true beauty.
Excellent stone for writers, musicians, artists, actors, sculptors,
        inventors, poets, dancers, and all other creative people.
Symbolizes artistic emotions, natural intuition, and all
        mental faculties centered within your Higher Self.

MYTHIC CRYSTAL

A Double Terminated Snow Quartz Crystal is called a Mythic Crystal. Snow Quartz is quartz crystal with large amounts of air, gas, or water trapped inside which gives the crystal a snowy appearance. Snow Quartz Crystals will sometimes have clear spaces within them, but on the whole you will not be able to see clearly into or through them. Snow Quartz is also sometimes called Milk or Milky Quartz.

The double termination of this crystal allows you to move backwards and forwards in Earth history to access the great myths of humanity and begin the exploration of their messages as they apply to you. Your Mythic Crystal can be used to trace the origins of your own personal myths and belief systems, supporting you while you resolve any conflicting belief patterns holding you back or impeding your present growth. These crystals can also be instrumental in helping you create the personal myth you would like to be living right now, making these excellent affirmation and creative visualization tools.

Mythic Crystals are good spiritual balance stones and outstanding meditation tools. They are great assistants for expanding your consciousness, shedding light on the inner meanings of life at a pace you are able to assimilate it. Myths themselves contain and conceal strong spiritual truths for humanity, and are believed by some authorities to be a necessary step in the overall development and evolution of human consciousness.

And since Snow Quartz Crystal is The Observation Stone, your Mythic Crystal can link you more directly to your powers of perception and observation and allow you to view your world with the appreciation, excitement, wonder, and innocence of a child once again.

MYTHIC CRYSTAL QUICK REFERENCE:

Symbolizes the myth, the inner meaning of Life.
Outstanding Dream Stone.
Stimulates personal creativity.
Helps you create your own heroic mythic journey.
A great affirmation tool.
Generates psychic energies.
A good channelling tool.
Enhances communication with your Higher and Inner Self.
Helps you trace the origins of your belief patterns, your personal myths.
Allows movement backward and forward in Earth-time to access her myths.
Helps you stay in tune with child-like innocence, wonder, and excitement.
A good tool when looking for the inner meaning in just about anything.
Allows you to observe and clarify your perception of a situation.
Symbolizes your return to seeing life through the eyes of an innocent child.

NEEDLE CRYSTAL

A Needle Crystal is a long, clear, extremely thin and narrow crystal. A Needle is approximately four times as long as it is wide, exceptionally fragile, and easily snapped in two. They are usually inexpensive but are becoming harder and harder to find, probably due to their exceptional fragility.

Needle Crystals are used to direct energy movement with precision to and from areas of the body or to other stones, to move energy around, or to remove energy knots from an area. Needles are often used by those involved in alternative healing processes for these purposes and are wonderfully effective when used at the body's acupuncture points (as are Selenite Needles).

Needles are also good energy boosters and telepathic communication tools. Look at the faces (facets) of your Needle Crystal to check for other forms (e.g., Receiver, Time Link, Isis, Generator). Your Needle will be especially expert at directing and focusing energy associated with the function of that particular crystal personality.

Needles are often used in crystal layout patterns to connect, focus, and direct specific energy patterns. Needle Crystals are also excellent focus points when you are creating something, or even trying to stitch it back together.

NEEDLE CRYSTAL QUICK REFERENCE:

Outstanding tool for alternative healers.
Can be used to help "stitch" scattered energy back together.
Good connecting rods in energy layout patterns.
Recommended for use at acupressure body points.

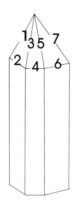

NUMEROLOGICAL CRYSTAL

Numerological Crystals are any and all quartz crystals with clearly defined facets (faces). Count the lines creating the outline of each face, add them up, and then reduce this number to a single digit just as you would any numerological computation. You will then be able to access and utilize more efficiently the power of the master number of your crystal.

For example, our illustration crystal has seven sides to its face. Since we are dealing with Flatland in our illustration, we need to double this number by counting all of the lines making up all of the faces around the crystal, to arrive at the number 14. Now add 1+ 4 and you have the number 5. Our illustration crystal has a master number of 5, and the number 5, among other things, symbolizes the human soul, sensual freedom, rapid change, and adventurousness—not a bad combination at all.

You can use this same method with any naturally faceted crystal, including your Crystal Clusters. When dealing with clusters, you can then either use each crystal individually or continue adding numbers until you arrive at a total master number for the cluster.

Being aware of the master number of your crystal is just one more way to maximize its use and benefits.

NUMEROLOGICAL CRYSTAL QUICK REFERENCE:

Amplifies the qualities of the master number contained in its facets.
Excellent channelling tool.
Special point of focus for the properties of its master number.

## OSIRIS CRYSTAL

An Osiris Crystal is any dark Smoky Quartz Generator Crystal, but it must be a natural Smoky Quartz, not one created by any mechanical process. A true Osiris will generally be so dark you cannot see through it, but you may be able to see deep into it. Your Osiris Crystal supports and protects you in all of your higher aspirations and is a direct link to your Higher Self.

Osiris as a symbol stands for the Higher Self and the First Logos. He was the "lord of all things" to the ancient Egyptians, born directly from the Word of God (the Logos) on the fifth day of creation and symbolizes Divine Love. Osiris is the creative energy of the Logos, the beginning of the duality of Spirit and Matter. He is often called the son of Space and Time (Seb and Mut), the firstborn of the five gods (the Five Planes of Existence). Osiris was associated by the Egyptians and other ancient cultures with Orion, while Isis was associated with the Sirius star system.

Since an Osiris is a Smoky Quartz Crystal, it automatically helps you maintain your desire to succeed in the physical world by restimulating any lost or misdirected human survival instincts. Your Osiris Crystal reminds you that one of your courses of study here on Earth is to learn to function effectively and powerfully within the physical dimension, a necessary course in your overall curriculum. Smoky Quartz Crystal also has the ability to contain and hold the highest level of light possible in a dark or black color. So in effect, your Smoky Quartz Osiris is time-released light and an extraordinary energy cleanser.

The Osiris Crystal is associated directly with the 1st chakra (the Base or Root Chakra) and all of its symbolism. An Osiris Crystal has the power to channel the light entering the 7th chakra in a smooth, downward spiral directly into the 1st chakra. This crystal is adept at helping you face, work with, and ultimately release any fears associated with letting go or holding on to anything or anyone too tightly or for too long.

An Osiris Crystal is obviously the perfect companion to an Isis Crystal, and together they symbolize the perfection of the Yin and Yang qualities, the Perfect Celestial Marriage.

## OSIRIS CRYSTAL QUICK REFERENCE:

Symbolizes the Higher Self descending into Matter.
Represents the creative energy of the Logos, the Creative Word.
A major Power Stone.
One of the Shaman Stones.
Excellent Dream Stone.
One of the Rescue Stones.
Reminds you that you are here partly to master being physical.
Stimulates a strong desire to succeed.
Strongly associated with and connected to the 1st chakra.
Superb channel for light from the 7th chakra to the 1st.
Rekindles any lost feelings of wanting to survive in the physical world.

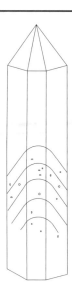

## PHANTOM CRYSTAL

A crystal which grows *completely over* another smaller crystal is called a Phantom Crystal. Looking into your crystal you will see one or more smaller crystal formations within the same framework. If a fully-formed crystal is growing out of another it is not a Phantom, it is an Inner Child. If a fully-formed crystal is growing completely inside the larger crystal it is not a Phantom, it is a Creator Crystal (see Creator and Inner Child Crystals).

The phantoms within your crystal usually appear wispy and ghost-like. The inner phantom crystals are sometimes hard to see and often have no hard or clearly-defined outlines. But they will always have the same basic structure of the larger outer crystal.

What actually happened to your Phantom is this: at some point several million years ago the crystal grew to a certain height and shape and then its nutritional source was shut off. Then at some later time, new solution flowed in and the crystal began to grow again, but totally within the boundaries of its original framework, rather than taking new forms or directions. In other words, the crystal grew beyond its original plan or expectations due to new incoming nutrients which provided the opportunity for continued growth and expansion within its original form. Focusing on a Phantom Crystal can remind you that you, too, can grow far beyond your expectations and that you are always well protected during these times of new growth. Just be patient and trust that your own additional nutrition will show up right on schedule exactly when you need it, in the quantities you need it or can assimilate.

Phantoms can be used in meditation or sleep to help you trace your essence through its many selves as far back as you care to go. They can also be used much as you would use an Inner Child Crystal, reminding you that the child within (the phantom) is always safe and protected. The outer crystal sheaths the inner phantoms very much like your Higher Self covers and shelters you. Your Phantom is also a good reminder that everything in your life started first with just a thought, an insubstantial wispy idea, before it was brought forward into a more solid reality.

Phantoms are found in all colors and shapes. The inner phantom will sometimes be an inclusion of a completely different mineral from its surrounding quartz (e.g., there are Chlorite Phantoms and Siderite Phantoms). Your Phantom Crystal then takes on all of the properties of itself and its inner mineral phantom.

PHANTOM CRYSTAL QUICK REFERENCE:

Symbolizes the Higher Self protecting the personality self.
Reminds you of your many spiritual levels of existence.
One of the Rescue Stones.
A good Dream Stone.
One of the Shaman Stones.
Helps alleviate grief and feelings of loss.
Outstanding meditation tool.
Excellent choice during transition and change.
Allows access to past and parallel life experiences and memories.
Stimulates psychic awareness.
Dissipates inner stresses.
Excellent companion when experiencing emotional traumas.
First rate protection stone.
Stimulates creativity and growth.
Promotes courage in thought and action.
Outstanding energy shield and protection stone.
Good nurturing stone.
Helps with lessons involving compassion.
A good choice when working with addictions.
Helps you accept being in the physical world.
A good tool when working with fear of personal power.
Helps alleviate depression and melancholy.
First rate protection stone for children.
Outstanding tool for working with lessons on patience.
Stimulates a strong desire to find your true origins.
A good reminder that you exist on many levels and in many forms.
Good communication device for talking with your teachers and guides.
Reminds you to stay connected to your Source and Higher Self.
Good tool for accessing and working with your belief systems.
Reminds you to grow beyond any self-limiting expectations.
Reminds you that even seemingly insubstantial dreams
        can become substantial reality.

PICTURE WINDOW CRYSTAL

Picture Window Crystals are slightly rounded, tumbled, egg-shaped pieces of quartz crystal originally found in the riverbeds of Brazil. These crystals were washed down out of the mountains and tumbled over and over by violently surging water. This natural treatment gives the Picture Window Crystal its characteristic frost-like outer covering.

One end of these crystals has been sliced off and polished to allow you to see deep into the crystal itself. Picture Window Crystals make one of the best open-eyed meditation tools, taking you with them deep into the crystal energy world. These are very powerful meditation tools when properly used and make good vision quest or Shaman Stones. Picture Window Crystals are exceptional tools when you are trying to open up to wider, clearer views, both inside and out.

PICTURE WINDOW CRYSTAL QUICK REFERENCE:

Symbolizes the process of going within to connect with Spirit.
Represents Peace and Harmony.
One of the Shaman Stones.
A good Dream Stone.
Excellent meditation tool.
A good stone for working with anxieties of all kinds.
A good tool for visualizing and experiencing crystal energies.
Helps you deal with lessons concerning loss, grief and physical death.
A good choice for communicating with your teachers.

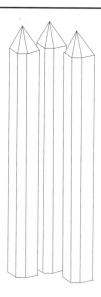

## QUANTUM CRYSTAL

Three or more quartz crystals of equal or nearly equal size and length naturally joined together create a Quantum Crystal. If all of the crystals in a Quantum are double terminated, their power is immeasurably increased.

Quantum Crystals have the power to influence what present quantum physics calls *probability waves*. Just before one probability wave collapses and another begins there is a gap or split second in which your thoughts and feelings can influence the *probable* or most likely outcome of a situation. In other words, a Quantum Crystal can be exceptionally useful in helping you alter the probable statistical outcome of any situation.

Quantum Crystals also represent the number 3. Three, among many other interpretations, symbolizes mysticism; the spiritual synthesis of a thing; the outcome of the harmonic actions of Unity (number 1) on Duality (number 2); the accumulated effect of the gathering together of spiritual forces; natural growth; creative power and energy; the end of a conflict; and learning to move forward within duality. Three is one of the numbers for the Human Soul and has always been viewed as a "heavenly" number.

Quantums should be used with extreme caution. Even more than with other crystals and minerals, be sure you know what your hidden agendas are. What you send out, consciously and subconsciously, is magnified by Quantums twenty-fold. Since energy always follows feelings, and especially feelings linked to thought which are often totally submerged within your subconscious, check and recheck your wish-list when working with your Quantum. Be sure you have said precisely what you mean because you can be sure that you *will* get exactly what you are concentrating on—no more, no less. And remember that this kind of energy does not speak nor necessarily understand plain English. Be specific!

## QUANTUM CRYSTAL QUICK REFERENCE:

Symbolizes the process of obtaining perfection while still within Matter.
Represents a gathering together of forces or energies.
One of the most potent Power Stones.
One of the Shaman Stones.
Excellent Dream Stone, especially if you are incubating a dream.
A good Rescue Stone.
Outstanding choice for affirmations and prayers.
Has the inherent ability to impact probability waves at the quantum level.
Excellent channelling device.
Outstanding energy booster and recharger.
Good choice for entrepreneurs.
Ignites and powers psychic energy.
Helps alleviate depression.
Good tool for accessing your belief systems.
A good telepathic communication device.
Good rebirthing tool.
Superior energy shield.
A good choice when you are ready to make conscious changes.
Helps you communicate more directly with your Higher or Inner Self.
Contains all of the symbolism of the number 3, multiplied.

## RAINBOW CRYSTAL

Rainbow Crystals are any form of quartz crystal which naturally flash the colors of the rainbow when turned in the light. The reflection of light creating the rainbow most often comes from an ancient crack in the crystal which allowed another mineral or water to flow into the crystal's interior. When light hits this inclusion it is reflected back from both sides. And since the rays reflected back from the two sides do not quite perfectly match, we are lucky enough to get the rainbow effect. Interestingly enough, really good quality Rainbow Quartz Crystal (also called Iris Quartz) is rarer than Diamonds.

Rainbow Crystals remind you to see the natural beauty all around you every moment, and that when you remember to tune in to Nature your life automatically becomes calmer, more rewarding, and better balanced. Rainbows remind you to lighten up, that your life is supposed to be fun, to not take things so seriously, and that being slightly out of alignment with your surroundings is not always a bad thing. Without this temporary imbalance you might miss your own rainbows.

Rainbow Crystals are natural promoters of happiness, hope, optimism, peace, courage, creativity, and respect for all life. These crystals are especially good for anyone who tends to spend too much time inside themselves. Remember that only light can cause a rainbow, and light has a hard time entering anything that is tightly closed. Rainbows cannot appear in total darkness, no matter what they do.

Rainbow Crystals are master depression fighters and encourage shy people to peek out and join the rest of the world. These are great emotional healers, making them one of the best Rescue Stones around.

Rainbow Crystals remind you that you have already weathered many storms and that you have the strength to make it through anything you must, anytime you must. They are excellent reminders that you are already a survivor. Rainbows show you that it is often the rough treatment you suffer from strong outside sources that open up a chink in your armor and allow the light to come in. They are prime examples of what you can accomplish when you decide to turn lemons into lemonade.

The rainbow itself is a strong symbol of the movement of Consciousness through the levels of growth which each color of the rainbow spectrum represents (i.e., your movement from red through violet). Rainbows are symbolic bridges between this world and the next in virtually all cultures, and rainbows of any kind are always strong symbols of transformation and the promise of new beginnings. Choose a Rainbow Crystal anytime you need to be reminded that there is no real separation between the higher and lower, the spiritual and the physical worlds.

RAINBOW CRYSTAL QUICK REFERENCE:

Symbolizes a divine promise or covenant.
Symbolizes the bridge between this world and the next.
Represents harmony between all states of consciousness.
Symbolizes the higher mental planes of existence.
A strong symbol of transformation and a better life to come.
Symbolizes regained good health and harmony.
A symbol of new beginnings and a new way of being.
One of the Rescue Stones.
Excellent Dream Stone.
Stimulates strong feelings of optimism and hope.
First rate anti-depression tool.
Assists in communication with your Higher Self.
Stimulates the courage to trust yourself enough to risk loving.
Reminds you to accept yourself for who you are, as you are.
Good choice when working with lessons concerning unconditional love.
Helps prevent emotional breakdowns.
Excellent tool when working with lessons connected with your parents.
Outstanding meditation tool.
Promotes self-confidence in naturally shy people.
Stimulates confident attitudes.
Calms and soothes what's wrong.
A good psychic energy stone.
Good divination stone.
Stimulates compassionate attitudes.
A good protection stone, especially during "stormy weather".
Aids in maintaining spiritual balance.
Creates a strong desire for harmony with others.
Cleanses and recharges its environment.
Helps you deal with lessons involving death of any kind.
Reminds you to keep your promises.
Dissipates apathetic attitudes.
Promotes the capacity to trust.
A good natural bridge between Spirit and Matter.
Reminds us that we are much more than we often believe we are.
Good choice to remind you there is no real separation between
        the spiritual and physical worlds.

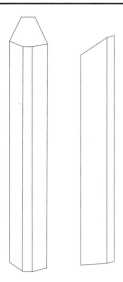

RECEIVER CRYSTAL

A quartz crystal with one broad, upward-sloping face (facet) is a Receiver Crystal, sometimes called a Receiving Crystal. These crystals are good for drawing out, moving, and receiving energy and are often used by healers involved with alternative healing procedures for this reason.

Holding a Receiver in your left hand and a Generator in your right is an excellent way to circulate energy through your body (often called "running energy") or to enhance or charge energy being sent. These crystals will allow you to receive just about any type of energy faster and smoother. Receivers are also good physical energy chargers and rechargers.

Receiver Crystals remind you to be more open and receiving, to accept new concepts and ideas, and to accept others more non-judgmentally and with fewer and fewer personal opinions blocking your view. They remind you it is as important to learn to receive as to give.

Receivers, of course, make great Dream Stones and meditation tools, and are the perfect partner for a Generator Crystal.

RECEIVER CRYSTAL QUICK REFERENCE:

Symbolizes your readiness to receive, as well as give.
A good Dream Stone.
Excellent divination stone.
First rate channelling tool.
Great tool for circulating energy.
Has the ability to draw out energy.

RECEIVER CRYSTAL continued:

Very calming and soothing in all its actions.
Reminds you to remain open to accepting new ideas and concepts.
Helps you be more open and non-judgmental of just about anything.
A good telepathic communication tool.
Helps to balance the hemispheres of the brain.
Especially sensitive to receiving all types of energy.
A good rebirthing stone.
Use anytime you want to be more flexible, open, and empathic.
Excellent choice for communicating with just about anything or anyone.
Perfect companion to a Generator Crystal.
Good choice when you want to be especially clear about
          what you are receiving.

RECEIVER-GENERATOR CRYSTAL

A Receiver-Generator Crystal is any Generator Crystal with one face (facet) that slopes inward more than its other five faces. In other words, it will not resemble a true Generator because all of its six faces are not perfectly equidistant from one another and do not come to a perfect point at the top-center (see Generator Crystal).

Receiver-Generators simultaneously receive and project energy patterns. These are obviously superior communication devices. They are great tools for anyone involved in transmuting energy and working with alternative forms of healing.

A Receiver-Generator is much easier to find than a true Generator, and the best news about that is that they are multi-functional tools—you get two for the price of one. This crystal is a superb divination and telepathic communication tool and will cleanse and recharge energy at the same time during these processes. It carries within it all of the symbolism and abilities of both a Receiver Crystal and a Generator Crystal. A Receiver-Generator would be an excellent choice for working with learning the delicate balance between receiving and giving.

RECEIVER-GENERATOR CRYSTAL QUICK REFERENCE:

Symbolizes balance between giving and receiving.
One of the Power Stones.
One of the Shaman Stones.
A good Dream Stone.

RECEIVER-GENERATOR continued:

One of the Rescue Stones.
Excellent telepathic communication tool.
Good energy shield.
Great tool for accessing your belief systems.
Enhances all forms of communication.
Helps alleviate depression and lack of self-esteem.
Exceptional energy recharger and transformer.
Helps you work with fears of all kinds.
Stimulates feelings of self-confidence.
A terrific "if you think you can, you can!" buddy.
Represents your ability to both give and receive with grace.

RECORD KEEPER CRYSTAL

Sometimes also called Recorders, Record Keeper Crystals are crystals with a geometric symbol (most often a triangle, but not always) *naturally* etched into one or more of its faces or sides. These geometric shapes are often not visible without searching for them under a good light and it is not unusual for them to show up after you have had your stone for awhile, in places where you know there weren't any before.

The geometric etchings or engravings are natural formations and can be felt by running your finger over the slight indentation or raised area of your crystal. Sometimes these geometric shapes are buried within the crystal, but most often they are somewhere on its surface.

Record Keepers are believed to contain stored information which can be accessed only by those who are at the same energy frequencies as the information. Only these individuals will be able to understand and interpret the data the crystal holds. As we said, it is not uncommon for a crystal you have had for some time to suddenly expose its record. The information will surface when your energy corresponds to the information stored. That is, in fact, the only way to access these ancient records, so don't give up.

Record Keepers are very personal crystals and attract the person meant to access and interpret their records. But do not expect the information to be in logical, left brain English. It may or may not "make sense" to you at the time. This is where trust comes into play, not to mention patience.

While we're talking about Record Keepers, keep in mind that any true geometric shape on a Record Keeper is a record. A crystal with several, or even all, of our currently recognized geometric shapes etched on or held inside them is a Master Matrix Crystal, the matrix from which other Record Keepers were originally programmed, and with which you can reboot deprogrammed ones (see Master Matrix Crystal).

Record Keepers should be treated with special reverence and respect, much as you would value an ancient book. The information a Record Keeper holds, by the way, does not have to be exalted or "spiritual" at all, but can be entirely practical, like where to locate a vital source of water in the wilderness. The key word here is information, which does not automatically or necessarily translate to "spiritual knowledge".

RECORD KEEPER QUICK REFERENCE:

Symbolizes your ability to expand your present base of knowledge.
Outstanding Dream Stone.
Holds and transmits ancient information and records.
Allows access to past and parallel life experiences and memories.
Expands your present information base.
Excellent spiritual attunement tool.
First rate divination stone.
Helps you work with fear of misuse of your personal power.
Outstanding meditation tool.
Enhances all forms of communication.
A good channelling device.
Helps you focus energy.
Reminds you that there is always something more to be learned.
A good tool for communicating with your guides, teachers, and Higher Self.
Reminds you to stay in tune with who you truly are.
Carries all of the symbolism of its geometric records.

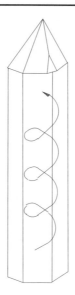

RIGHT HANDED CRYSTAL

A quartz crystal with an extra facet (face) on the right side of the largest facet of the crystal is a Right Handed Crystal. This simply means that the energy spiral in the crystal flows naturally to the right, and even mineralogists don't always agree on why this should be so (see page 2).

Right Handed Crystals help activate the logical, intellectual, verbal left side of the brain. These are excellent tools to use for any activity requiring analytical and intellectual abilities, or for working on ego-related problems.

Right Handed Crystals encourage you to study and learn. These are a good choice for students of all kinds and make an excellent balance for Left Handed Crystals. Right Handed Crystals are also a good choice for balancing excessive Yin (female) energies.

As a symbol, the right *generally* represents the Yang (male) principle, generosity, power, creativity, assertiveness and aggression, physical responsibilities, and the ability to intellectually understand symbols. You can use your Right Handed Crystal to help you with any of these things. They are perfect companions for Left Handed Crystals.

RIGHT HANDED CRYSTAL QUICK REFERENCE:

Symbolizes all left brain activities.
Represents Yang (male) energies.
Good companion and balance for a Left Handed Crystal.
Helps you work with ego-related issues.
Aids in the decision making process.

RIGHT HANDED CRYSTAL continued:

Enhances your verbal expression abilities.
Directly activates the action centers of the brain.
Good choice for students of all kinds.
Stimulates the intellect and logic.
Generates psychic energy.
Balances excessive Yin (female) energies.
A good telepathic communication tool.
Boosts powers of concentration.
A good channelling tool.
Balances the hemispheres of the brain when used with a Left Handed Crystal.
Good choice when trying to regain and maintain mental balance.
Connects you more directly to the left side of the brain.
Carries all of the symbolism of the right.
Can be used to slow down or speed up the energies of the left brain.
Symbolizes all interpretations of the Left.

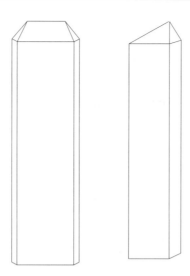

SCANNER CRYSTAL

A Scanner Crystal is a crystal with one or more wide flat sides. Many Scanner Crystals have only one wide, flat, tabular side, their other sides being more in conformance with the usual shape of a quartz crystal. Scanners are generally not Tabbies, but of course may be, especially since many Scanners do not have well-defined terminations (points). They also seem to appear more as Receivers than Generators, but this also is not a given.

Scanner Crystals are used to scan the energy systems of just about anything. Simply hold your scanner in your left hand (unless you are more sensitive to energy through your right) and move it slowly over the object or person to be scanned, holding it approximately one to two inches from the physical surface.

Any images or impressions you receive while scanning the person or object are held and retained within the Scanner Crystal until you are ready to clear it, increasing your capacity to reaccess any impressions or information after any energy work. This is especially useful when you are in a situation where multiple impressions are coming at you or when you need to focus on only one prominent issue at the time of scanning.

Scanners are terrific assistants and help you get a much clearer picture or feeling about any energy work you are doing. They are often used by those involved in alternative healing procedures for just this reason. A Scanner Crystal is an excellent tool for locating exactly where the body or energy field is experiencing its most sluggish energy flow. Scanners are also used to smooth energy, helping to gently but firmly unwind any knots or rough spots encountered in energy fields.

Scanner Crystals are not necessarily attractive and very often have many inclusions or areas of trapped ancient air or gases, lending them a slightly snowy and used look. Although the very best Scanners are perfectly clear, they are incredibly rare and often expensive.

Scanners can be any other crystal personality in addition to being a Scanner (e.g., Receiver, Time Link, Isis, etc.). If you are lucky enough to find Scanners in different forms, you will be able to choose the most appropriate tool for the job at hand. For example, if you wanted to scan yourself or someone else for any energy knots or blocks related to the past, you might want to use a Time Link Scanner rather than a Comet Scanner.

SCANNER QUICK REFERENCE:

A good Rescue Stone.
Superior tool for smoothing out energy kinks or knots.
Lets you locate sluggish or blocked energies points.
Helps you scan and interpret energy of the object or person being scanned.
Stores scanned information for later retrieval.

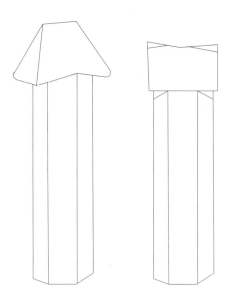

SCEPTER QUARTZ CRYSTAL

Scepter Quartz Crystal is a crystal with an overgrowth capping its termination (point). The cap is actually a younger crystal which grew over the top of the older one. Scepter Crystals very much resemble the royal scepters carried by kings and queens. Scepters are not the same as Phantom or Creator Crystals (see Phantom Crystal, Creator Crystal).

Scepter Crystals directly link the 7th, 8th, 9th, and 10th chakras, facilitating a smoother, cleaner flow of energy between them. Scepters also remind us of who we really are—the sons and daughters of spiritual royalty. Use or carry a Scepter Crystal anytime you need to be more closely in touch with your true essence and anytime you need to make sure you are acting from your true Self, not from your personality, ego, or the needs of your physical body.

Scepters themselves symbolize sovereignty, authority, divine or royal power and authority to rule. They are strong phallic symbols as well of course. Scepters are and always have been associated with all sky deities. To the ancient Buddhists, the Diamond Scepter symbolized the highest power of the Buddha, while the early Christians associated the scepter with the Archangel Gabriel. And to the ancient Hindu, a scepter represented *dharma*, the Highest Authority upholding Cosmic Order.

## SCEPTER CRYSTAL QUICK REFERENCE:

Symbolizes Divine Authority.
Represents transmission of the Life Force.
Symbolizes new information capping and authenticating old.
One of the Rescue Stones.
Excellent Dream Stone.
Reminds you who you really are and where you originated.
Excellent channelling device.
Establishes a firm connection to Spirit and your own true essence.
A good fertility stone.
Generates psychic energy.
Superior protection stone.
Good telepathic communication tool.
Great confidence builder and booster.
Stimulates the courage to take action and follow through.
Directly links the 7th, 8th, 9th and 10th chakras.
Allows more direct communication with your Higher Self.
Good reminder of your responsibilities toward all life.
Reminds you to be more aware of your actions,
        especially as they impact others.

SCRUBBER CRYSTAL

Scrubber Crystals are Crystal Clusters of any size whose points are all of even and equal, or nearly equal, length. Scrubbers look like crystal scrub brushes, which pretty much describes what they do.

You can use your Scrubber to literally scrub down the energy around your body. Holding your Scrubber in your hand and using any scrubbing motion you prefer (back and forth, circular, up and down), scrub the area one to two inches from your physical body. Keep scrubbing until you feel your energy begin to change. The reaction is usually immediate, but don't worry if it takes longer. Many people find the area just back of their spine is most sensitive, but experiment. These are energy scrubbers only and are never used to touch or scrub the physical body.

Scrubbers are especially beneficial when you feel a cold coming on or need a quick energy fix between meetings. Keep one in your shower to help power up; the combination of running water and crystal energy in motion is quite an experience.

Scrubbers, even more than other crystals, should be cleansed and recharged often.

SCRUBBER CRYSTAL QUICK REFERENCE:

Scrubs, cleanses, and revitalizes the energies surrounding the physical body.
Aids in the coordination of your physical energies.
Outstanding energy booster.
Good choice for children.
Highly recommended for use before any healing procedures.
Contains all of the capacities of a Crystal Cluster.

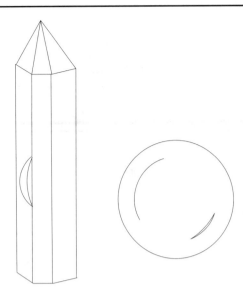

SELENE CRYSTAL

Selene Crystals are named for Selene, ancient goddess of the moon (sometimes spelled *Celene* by earlier cultures). A Selene Crystal is any crystal with a rounded inner inclusion somewhere within it reminiscent of the various phases of the moon. The natural curve inside the crystal can be a complete circle, representing the full moon; a semi-circle, representing the half moon; or a small sliver, representing the quarter, waning, and new moon.

Meditating with a Selene Crystal will help you connect more directly with your intuitive, sensitive, compassionate, nurturing qualities. A Selene can help you keep a closer connection to your Yin (female) qualities and nature, whether you are female or male.

This crystal is very soothing and calming and an excellent Dream Stone when placed by your bed or under your pillow, promoting sound, restful sleep and peaceful dreams.

Since this stone is associated with the moon and all moon deities, a Selene Crystal would make a good gift for both women and men having trouble expressing, experiencing, or allowing their Yin qualities to show, especially those of us who have trouble getting in touch with and expressing our feelings.

Selene Crystals stimulate and amplify your natural psychic abilities, insight into the Mysteries, and your direct connection to your Inner Self, all while keeping you in closer touch with your real feelings.

Selene was the Mother of the Universe, the Eternal Great Mother, the Eternal One, First Woman, and the Cause and Measurer of Time, the one who created time and the cycles of Creation. The moon itself was often seen as the Mirror of the Goddess, which reflected everything within the physical world. Selene was one of the many aspects of Aphrodite, Hathor, Astarte, Artemis, Diana, Isis, Venus, and all other moon deities, both female and male.

The Moon has always been an emblem of the Great Mother and all Queens of Heaven, and was often addressed as "Beloved of the Sun" and "Eye of the Night". As a symbol in its own right, the Moon represents all cycles and rhythms; the becoming of a thing within its own timing; birth-death-resurrection; psychic and intuitive awareness; love; peace; the unconscious or subconscious mind; the emotions; magic; mysticism; the Vital Spirit which holds Body and Soul together; the involuntary and instinctual nature and instincts; and sensual attunement to physical chemical cycles. It has always been seen as the Controller of Destiny and Time, the Weaver of Fate.

As an object which cannot generate light by its own power but can only shine through its reflection from the source of light (the Sun), your Selene Crystal symbolizes your willingness to follow, bask in, and always reflect the Light, just like the Moon.

SELENE CRYSTAL QUICK REFERENCE:

Symbolizes all Moon deities, male and female.
Represents the natural Cycles of Creation.
Symbolizes timing and allowing things to happen in their own time.
An excellent Dream Stone.
A good Rescue Stone.
Greatly heightens your natural intuition.
Amplifies your psychic awareness and energy.
Stimulates a strong desire for self-reflection.
Softens excessive Yang (masculine) energy and characteristics.
Heightens all Yin (feminine) energy and characteristics.
Dramatically enhances creativity, especially through your feelings.
Promotes sound, peaceful, restful sleep.
Helps you deal with anger and frustration.
A good spiritual balance stone.
Good choice when dealing with your ego.
A great tool for gaining insight into "the Mysteries".
Keeps you firmly connected to your Inner Self.
Helps women be more comfortable with their femininity.
Aids men in getting in touch with their feelings and naturally sensitive natures.
One of the many emblems of Isis and other Queens of Heaven.
Excellent companion during transitions and cycles.
Helps you be more comfortable with changes as they occur.
Good comforter during the full moon.
Reminds you that all life moves continually through cycles
        and is in a constant state of changing form.
Assists in communicating with your teachers
        (especially when used with Pyrite).

## SELF HEALED CRYSTAL

A Self Healed Crystal is a quartz crystal which was severed from its original matrix or cluster while still in the Earth. Then at some later time new solution poured in over the fractured end and the crystal began to grow new crystals over the break, in effect healing its own wounds. Self Healed Crystals have survived major natural shake-ups over which they had no control and have managed to make the best of the situation, used the shake-up or potential disaster to transform themselves into a new, more productive personality.

This type of crystal is an excellent choice for someone in need of any type of healing—physical, emotional, mental, or spiritual. Self Healed Crystals are exceptionally supportive for those of us with strong emotional issues or traumas, or who are struggling with some type of addiction. And addictions include the inability to let go of a certain kind of behavior, a person, or belief as well as tobacco, food, alcohol and drugs.

Self Healed Crystals are vivid tangible reminders that you have the ability to not only heal your wounds yourself, but also have the gift of being able to strengthen and beautify yourself in the process, to become much more than you were before you experienced the trauma. They remind you that separation from your original Source neither lessens nor threatens you and that you are a separate and total entity in your own right, able to function on your own even when severely wounded.

## SELF HEALED CRYSTAL QUICK REFERENCE:

Symbolizes your natural ability to heal yourself, no matter what.
One of the major Rescue Stones.
Aids in resisting the natural physical effects of aging.
A good companion during times of deep grief and loss.
Helps you kick addictions of any kind.
Good tool when working with feelings of guilt for any reason.
Highly recommended for all traumas.
Fights stresses, including those over which you have no control.
Good tool when working with weight control lessons.
Stimulates courage in action.
Excellent energy recharger.
Excellent energy shield.
Assists in dealing with fears of all kinds.
Good choice for anyone dealing with the effects of any type of abuse.
A good reminder that we are always ultimately responsible for your reactions.
Excellent choice during any cleansing procedures.
Represents your Higher Self interpreting wisdom gained through action and
	the experiences of living.
Reminds you that you are still whole, even when physically separated
	from your original source.

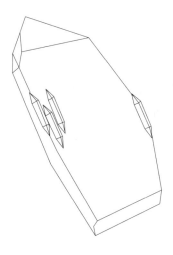

## SHARD CRYSTAL

Crystal Shards are flat, broad slices of quartz crystal which originally formed in layered, plate-like masses rather than in the usual six-sided hexagonal crystal shape. Shards can be either pieces of quartz crystal that have sheared off from their original source, or crystals which have chosen to form in this unusual angular, flat shape. Shards come in all sizes and shapes and can be either perfectly clear or snowy, with many smaller crystals growing on or from them. For instance, they often have Tabbies sprouting off one or more of their sides. Some are also Self Healed Crystals, and many Shards are Quantums. Shards are extremely versatile in their symbolism and functions.

A Shard Crystal is a good choice for crystal layout patterns when working with various alternative healing procedures, especially when working with the energy centers of the body, the chakras. Shard Crystals make good Dream Stones and are excellent meditation tools. And just like pottery shards, Shard Crystals can fit together to show you their original form or pattern.

There is something particularly soothing but energizing about all Shards, so play with them and take notes of your experiences with them. A fairly recent crystal personality, the Shard Crystal is a good candidate for experimentation to discover all of what it can do.

Shards remind you that you don't have to grow in normal, preplanned, expected patterns to have value and beauty. They can even tell you that being wide and flat ain't all bad. So keep stretching—you may surprise yourself at what you can become.

## SHARD CRYSTAL QUICK REFERENCE:

Symbolizes the freedom to be who and what you are.
A good Rescue Stone.
A good Dream Stone.
Wonderful meditation tool.
Calms and soothes while energizing.
Good choice when working with the chakra centers.
A reminder to keep stretching yourself.
Reminds you that being sheared off from your original Source
only opens new directions for creative growth and productivity.

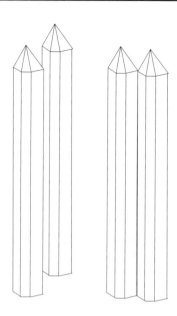

SOUL MATE CRYSTAL
Two quartz crystals of equal length and size growing side-by-side are Soul Mate Crystals. The crystals do not need to be perfectly aligned side-by-side so long as they are of equal length and size. In other words one can be standing on slightly lower ground than the other, but they are both really the same length.

While a soul mate is generally defined as someone who will be the "love of your life", we all have several soul mates not just one, and soul mates are not always connected (in human terms) through loving relationships. A soul mate is anyone with whom you have an unshakable deep connection at the soul level and is an entity who loves you so deeply and strongly that he/she will do whatever is necessary to facilitate and promote your spiritual growth. Most of us know by now that this is not necessarily a pleasant experience, although it is always a productive one.

In some systems of belief, a soul mate is one-half of a whole unit of consciousness who split itself into two for specific spiritual evolutionary purposes, while other systems support the belief that you have literally hundreds, even thousands, of soul mates. But no matter which of these two beliefs are yours, your Soul Mate Crystal will help you focus on connecting with a soul mate, someone who will be helpful in your life and growth at the time.

Soul Mate Crystals are excellent meditation and Dream Stones, helping you to get in contact with and begin to integrate your various selves so you may ultimately reunite with your Essence or Soul (especially when used with Halite).

101

## SOUL MATE CRYSTAL QUICK REFERENCE:

Symbolizes reuniting with your other half, your soul mate.
Excellent Dream Stone.
Helps you attract one of your many soul mates.
Great telepathic communication tool.
Enhances your natural sensuality.
Assists access to past and parallel life experiences and memories.
Enhances compatibility between energies.
Superb meditation stone.
A good choice when working with maintaining balance.
Exceptional channelling tool.
Enhances communication between any dual energies.
Good divination stone.
Generates psychic energy.
Helps you deal with fear of involvement and relationships, in any form, especially when used with Smithsonite.
Connects you more directly to the various personalities of your own Essence, especially when used with Halite.

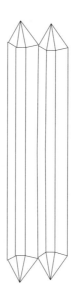

SPIRIT GUARDIAN CRYSTAL

Two Double Terminated Crystals of equal or nearly equal size and length growing side-by-side are called Spirit Guardian Crystals. These are very personal crystals and should be treated with much respect and honor.

Spirit Guardian Crystals help you remember that you are never, ever totally alone or abandoned, nor are you expected to accomplish all of your tasks without help. Spirit Guardians remind you that it's okay to ask for help, and not just for "spiritual" help. Spiritual Guardians love being practical, too.

Meditating with a Spirit Guardian Crystal connects you more directly to your spirit guardians, guides, and teachers on other levels of existence. This crystal will generally not be as effective at connecting you to any Earth-energy guardians (you might want to try an Apache Tear for that one) as it will be in connecting you more directly with your other-dimensional guardians.

In many belief systems a Guardian is a highly evolved Soul entrusted with sacred knowledge, while a Guide is a highly evolved Etheric World Intelligence who has lived many incarnations and who now provides guidance, assistance, protection, and psychic information, and who can communicate "hidden" or "secret" knowledge. Your Spiritual Guardian Crystal will connect you more directly to both of these sources.

SPIRIT GUARDIAN CRYSTAL QUICK REFERENCE:

Symbolizes spiritual protection.
One of the Power Stones.
One of the Rescue Stones.
An excellent Dream Stone.
Generates and helps maintain energy levels.
Aligns you more correctly with sacred knowledge.
Excellent tool during psychic development exercises.
Allows you access to "hidden" ancient knowledge and wisdom.
One of the best protection stones available.
One of the best channelling tools.
Reminds you that you have not been abandoned, and never will be.
Especially recommended as protection for infants and small children.
Superior energy shield.
Connects you more directly to your teachers, spirit guides, and guardians.
Reminds you that you are not expected to complete your tasks without help.
Tangible reminder to ask for help when you really need it.

TABULAR CRYSTAL

A Tabular Crystal is a quartz crystal with a flattened tabular shape; two of its opposite sides are twice as wide, or more, than its other sides. Often called Tabbies, these are the communication experts of the Crystal Clan. Tabbies enhance the communication and integration between all types of energies, and balance and smooth those energies as they flow through the Tabbie. Having Tabular Crystals around almost guarantees a productive exchange of energies within your Tabby's energy range, and this includes people (and especially when paired with a piece of Pyrite).

Tabbies literally bridge the communication gap between the human heart and mind, and help you translate your feelings into mental awareness and verbal expression. While Tabbies will not help break up old mental patterns, they are excellent bridges over the distances between the "higher" and "lower" and the inner and outer elements of yourself, and between your conscious and subconscious minds. In short, think *bridge* and *communication* when you see a Tabbie.

TABULAR CRYSTAL QUICK REFERENCE:

Symbolizes the bridge between the Heart and Mind.
The Communication Expert of the Crystal Clan.
An excellent Dream Stone.
A good Rescue Stone.
Outstanding at bridging and balancing the emotions.
Creates a bridge for communication between Matter and Spirit.

## TABULAR CRYSTAL CONTINUED:

Enhances the productive flow of energy of all kinds.
Excellent channelling device.
Helps bridge your climb from one level to the next.
Bridges the gap between the Inner and Outer Self.
Creates a bridge between the 4th, 5th and 6th chakras.
Calming and soothing in all of its actions.
Helps ease unreasonable fears.
First rate stress fighter.
Bridges the gap between your feelings and your verbal expression of them.
Superb connecting link in any programs or crystal layouts.
Provides for smoother communication between
        the conscious and subconscious.
Automatically strengthens and enhances all forms of communication,
        especially when boosted by Pyrite.

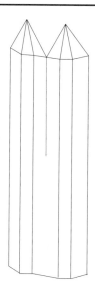

TANTRIC TWIN CRYSTAL

Tantric Twin Crystals are crystals who share a common base but who have two separate and distinct points (terminations). They are literally two heads on one body. The terminations on a Tantric Twin may or may not be of the same length or height but they must be born from a common base or body. These are not two side-by-side individual crystals, but one crystal with two points. Tantric Twins are not Soul Mates or Spirit Guardians (see Soul Mate Crystal, Spirit Guardian Crystal). Some Tantric Twins are also called Japanese Twins and are exact mirror images of one another.

The word *tantra* itself is an ancient Sanskrit word meaning *union.* Your most important union is always first with your True Self. The ultimate union is when your Soul becomes one with your Original Source, however you personally see that—as the Life Force, All That Is, the Tao, or God.

Tantric Twins work diligently and single-mindedly to help you with human relationships of all kinds. They prepare you to allow your twin essence or soul mate into your life at a very high energy level. (See Soul Mate, Twin Flame Crystal).

Tantric Twins are extraordinarily effective when working with the bonding of two individuals who are already intimately connected, and a Tantric Twin is one of the best choices for two people who are already deeply united and wish to explore and strengthen that bond even further.

Use your Tantric Twin just as you would any tantric tool or procedure, including sexual bonding. Employed effectively, a Tantric Twin will lead you into the discipline of tantra, the true aim of which is to free the spark of Divine Light hidden within each human being, including you. You can also use a Tantric Twin to help you see through the illusions of Time and Space and begin the process of understanding the nonspatial concepts of Nirvana, a place of awareness totally devoid of content, the place of Non-Being.

TANTRIC TWIN CRYSTAL QUICK REFERENCE:

Symbolizes union with the One, the All.
Represents the Spiritual Lover.
One of THE Power Stones—use with caution.
Excellent Dream Stone.
Helps you attract and hold on to love.
Aids in achieving union with your Higher Self.
Enhances compatibility between individuals.
Stimulates and magnifies your natural sensuality on all levels, not just sexual.
Good meditation stone for lovers.
An excellent energy shield.
Helps you learn to deal with all relationships at a more realistic level.
Provides you with a mirror of your other half, your twin essence.
Helps you learn to hold and then more productively release energy.
An excellent choice when working with lessons concerning human sexuality.
Leads you toward the release of the spark of Divine Light or energy within.

TEACHER CRYSTAL

When you look into one of your quartz crystals you will sometimes see a shape or form of some kind, often resembling a human figure, an animal, or even a mythical or abstract form. These crystals are called Teacher Crystals and can also be any other crystal personality. Often Teachers have more than one teacher within them, and these inner teachers can, and do, change. It is highly likely that one person's Teacher Crystal will not be another person's at all. These are personal and specific images or symbols meant for the individual attracted to them.

Meditation with a Teacher Crystal allows you a more direct access and connection to the information transmitted by your teacher. Your teachers, of course, are not physically living in the crystal but are projecting a portion of their energy there for your benefit and learning, choosing those symbols and shapes they know you will respond to best. Calm that little hamster running crazily around in your mental cage, teach yourself to quietly listen with no preconceived ideas or expectations, and your Teacher Crystal will begin to help you find exactly what you need to know when you need to know it, which direction might be preferable at the time, and even what you might like to be working on at the inner level.

Remember that the teachers in your Teacher Crystal are symbolic and you can interpret them just as you would any other personal symbol. At the very least, focusing on the shapes you see in your Teacher Crystal will help you become more creative, and certainly better in touch with your own symbols and understanding of them.

TEACHER CRYSTAL QUICK REFERENCE:

Symbolizes the inner teacher.
One of the Shaman Stones.
Superior Dream Stone.
A good Rescue Stone.
Stimulates psychic awareness and development.
Activates teaching dreams and visions.
Superb meditation stone.
Enhances self-awareness.
Helps you recognize and interpret your personal symbols.
A very good "listening" stone.
Good choice during a vision quest.
Good divination stone.
Excellent protection stone.
Almost always soothing and calming in its actions.
Stimulates and boosts creativity.
Allows easier communication with your guides and teachers.
Supports your work with lessons concerning your belief systems.
Helps you learn patience and trust.

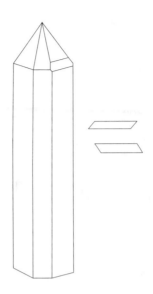

TIME LINK CRYSTAL

A quartz crystal with a parallelogram as one of its faces (facets) is a Time Link Crystal. The parallelogram itself is an ancient symbol for the power to emerge from your present position through the flexibility and willingness to learn and accept new ideas and new directions. If the parallelogram on your Time Link leans toward the left, it supports you in achieving your goals. If the parallelogram leans toward the right, it is a superb tool for igniting your natural inspiration and creativity.

Meditating or sleeping with a Time Link Crystal helps you begin to unravel the intellectual problems concerned with your personal concepts of Time. Time Links are also useful when tracing the evolution of your essence throughout your involvement within physical Time.

Time Links make excellent telepathic communication tools since they both understand Time and are able to work both inside and outside Time's limiting influences.

Time Link Crystals should be used and treated with awareness of what they represent. Does yours lean right or left? As with all information you receive with crystals, be sure you really want to know and are ready for the information. And be specific and clear in the way you ask.

## TIME LINK CRYSTAL QUICK REFERENCE:

Symbolizes your ability to emerge from your present state of being.
Represents your willingness to learn and to grow.
One of the Shaman Stones.
Excellent Dream Stone, especially for incubating dreams.
Excellent channelling tool.
First rate tool during past and parallel life recall exercises.
Good choice as a divination tool.
Helps you be more comfortable with being held within physical Time.
Reminds you to be patient and give yourself "time".
Allows you to see the illusions and lessons connected with Time.
Connects the past, present, and future related to Time.
Supports you while accessing parallel realities located within physical Time.
A good tool for working with lessons concerning physical death.
Good choice when working toward a goal (left-leaning parallelogram).
Ignites creativity and inspiration (right-leaning parallelogram).
Assists you in working out problems associated with
       your personal concepts of Time.

TONING CRYSTAL

A Toning Crystal is most often found as a long, often thin, *perfectly clear* quartz crystal, either single or double terminated. Most, if not all, of the angles on a Toning Crystal are at right angles to one another or slightly curved at right angles. Toning Crystals are not Laser Crystals; all Lasers have a slightly used, ancient look, while Toning Crystals often appear to be almost manmade, even when they are still in their natural state (see Laser Crystal).

While Toning Crystals are usually long and thin, some crystals which originally were Toning Crystals may by now have been shaped into Crystal Spheres or other handworked shapes, so don't miss them. Some authorities believe that true Toning Crystals were created and programmed in ancient Lemuria for the specific purpose of teaching and healing through sound.

Toning Crystals are used to intensify, amplify, and store sound. These crystals are often preprogrammed by chanting, speaking, singing, or playing specific music or sounds directly into them. While all quartz crystal has the ability to take in, hold, transform, and transmit frequencies, Toning Crystals are the sound experts of the Crystal Clan and are often used in alternative healing procedures using sound.

Regular practice with your Toning Crystal will increase your sensitivity and response to sound frequencies, light frequencies, and even the energy spin within your chakras. It provides an excellent homing signal during out-of-body exercises, especially when paired with Lapis Lazuli.

Toning Crystals function as a bridge between Earth's root civilizations and the home planet from which each originated. They are also excellent bridges between the Inner and Outer Worlds, your inner and outer selves.

TONING CRYSTAL QUICK REFERENCE:

Symbolizes the bridge of sound between the Inner and Outer Worlds.
The sound frequency expert of the Crystal Clan.
A good tool for increasing your sensitivity to sound and other frequencies.
Excellent affirmation tool.
Holds and transmits sound frequencies.
Good choice for meditation.
Supports out-of-body travel through sound.
Best choice when experimenting with light and sound.
The best crystal tool for experimenting with sound frequencies.
Superior tool for alternative healers.
Believed to help create a bridge between Earth's root races and
their original home planets or systems.
Believed to have been created and programmed in Lemuria for
very specific healing and teaching purposes.

TRANSMITTER CRYSTAL

A Transmitter Crystal is a quartz crystal with two symmetrical 7-sided facets (faces) on both sides of a triangular 3-sided face. The triangle will always be in the center of the crystal's facets, with a 7-sided facet on either side of it.

Transmitters represent the mathematical ratio 7:3:7, symbolizing personal power (the number 3) held in balance by the energy of Perfect Order (the two 7's). Transmitter Crystals are excellent tools for clarifying, simplifying, and refining your ability to communicate with just about anything on just about any level.

Transmitters are also often Record Keeper Crystals with specific information for specific individuals (see Record Keeper Crystal). They are slightly more Yang (masculine) in their actions and should always be used with their termination pointed up. Transmitters are believed to connect the Third Dimension directly to higher dimensions of existence.

Transmitter Crystals connect your conscious mind to the Universal or Soul Mind. These make superior manifestation and affirmation tools as long as you are perfectly clear about what you are transmitting, because you will get precisely what you asking for, in precisely the way you are asking for it. This crystal is also an excellent Dream Stone and a good telepathic communication tool. Transmitters intensify your intuitive abilities and then help you integrate what you learn.

A Transmitter is an excellent check-and-balance tool, allowing you to become more comfortable with your inner personal power as it strengthens and develops. They also, of course, pick up the symbolism of 3 and 7.

TRANSMITTER CRYSTAL QUICK REFERENCE:

Symbolizes Trust at the cosmic or spiritual level.
Symbolizes your personal power held in perfect balance by your spiritual power.
Excellent Dream Stone.
Stimulates and intensifies your natural intuitive abilities.
Outstanding telepathic communication tool.
Good choice as an affirmation tool.
Excellent support when working with personal power lessons.
Connects your conscious mind more directly with the Soul or Universal Mind.
Helps you clarify, simplify, and refine your communication skills.
Connects the Third Dimension directly to the Universal Mind energies.
Represents personal power held in balance by Perfect Order
and Celestial Harmony.

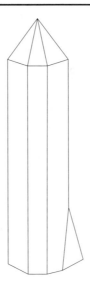

TRIGGER CRYSTAL

A crystal with a smaller crystal on one of its sides near its base is a Trigger Crystal, but some triggers are found farther up the crystal's body. In many cases the smaller crystal at the base is not fully formed and resembles a slope reaching up the base or side of the crystal. While our illustration shows a Generator Trigger, Triggers can be any crystal personality. So you may find an Isis Trigger, a Time Link Trigger, a Receiver Trigger, etc. (However, if you have an Osiris Trigger, you might want to make sure it's not loaded when you point it, just to be safe).

When pressed, the smaller crystal trigger fires a focused, concentrated, enormously amplified burst of energy through the termination (point) of the larger crystal. Trigger Crystals are often used by those working in alternative healing fields to focus and concentrate energy to a specific spot, and should always be used only with training and knowledge.

Trigger Crystals allow short, intense bursts of energy to be injected more precisely into any stone program or for any other purpose for which you may be using your Trigger. These are major protection stones and excellent go-anywhere, "I'll take care of you" buddies.

TRIGGER CRYSTAL QUICK REFERENCE:

Symbolizes intense, powerful, focused energy.
Projects pooled and focused energy in short, intense bursts.
Enhances your decision-making abilities.
Helps dissolve personal illusions.
Sparks a strong desire for independence.

TRIGGER CRYSTAL continued:

Dissolves unconscious insecurities impeding your movement.
A good meditation and thought form booster.
Helps you discover your personal lessons.
First rate protection stone.
Stimulates feelings of self-confidence.
Good tool when dealing with fears of all kinds.
Holds and transmutes energies.
Outstanding tool for alternative healers.
Takes on all the qualities of its crystal personality formation.

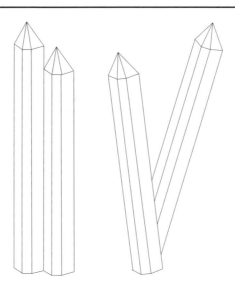

TWIN FLAME CRYSTAL

Twin Flame Crystals are two crystals of similar, but not equal, length and size joined either at their base in a V shape or joined at their sides. Twin Flames are not Soul Mates. Soul Mates are of equal or nearly equal size and length (see Soul Mate Crystal).

Focusing on a Twin Flame Crystal helps you attract people whose spiritual evolvement is compatible with yours, kindred souls on a platonic rather than romantic or sexual level. Your twin flame can be a brother, sister, friend, benefactor, boss, coworker, teacher, child, parent, or just someone who shows up briefly and mysteriously one day.

Twin Flame Crystals function as mirrors for how you appear on an inner level to the outside world. Twin Flames clearly show you who you are and how you feel about it at the moment. Twin Flame Crystals are terrific tools for gaining and then maintaining psychic connection to your own twin flames who show up with just the right words or ideas when you need them most.

TWIN FLAME CRYSTAL QUICK REFERENCE:

Symbolizes *like attracting like*.
Attracts compatible spiritual companions.
An excellent communication stone, especially telepathic.
Attracts platonic love relationships.
Aids in accessing past and parallel life information and memories.

TWIN FLAME CRYSTAL continued:

Channels twin flame energy patterns.
Boosts your natural capacity to create compatible relationships.
Excellent tool for building psychic affinity with others.
Helps you see how you present your inner feelings to the outside world.
Assists you in becoming comfortable with unrecognized qualities of yourself
through more active involvement with others.

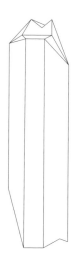

WARRIOR CRYSTAL

Warrior Crystals are quartz crystal power pieces (most often Generators, Lasers, or Quantums) which have been harshly handled and consequently have damaged, chipped, or broken points. Warrior Crystals symbolize the spiritual warrior in you and remind you that you are expected to overcome anything blocking your growth without complaining, even if life drops you on your head a few times. Warriors are not Empaths; they have not been that badly damaged (see Empathic Crystal).

Warrior Crystals often display brilliant rainbows, and it is often the effort of overcoming the damage to their power that has caused the Warrior to create and reflect back these rainbows. Warriors remind us to do the same (see Rainbow Crystal).

These crystals are excellent strengtheners of your mental and spiritual qualities and connect you more directly to the Earth's energies surrounding you at any given moment, wherever you are. Warriors are great companions on any part of your spiritual journey or quest.

Meditation with Warrior Crystals can help you access your own spiritual warrior nature and, with the proper effort on your part, even lead you to your vision quest and support you on your journey.

In short, Warriors help you access your warrior qualities and remind you that the only battle you ever really fight is with your own nature. Warriors remind you to take responsibility for your life and your reactions to it, and to see your excuses for not being your true self for what they really are. Then your Warrior makes sure you overcome any illusions and self-limitations with truth, integrity, and absolute impeccability.

WARRIOR CRYSTAL QUICK REFERENCE:

Symbolizes personal truth, integrity, and the ability to live impeccably.
Symbolizes the spiritual warrior.
One of the Power Stones.
One of the Shaman Stones.
A good Dream Stone.
Excellent Rescue Stone.
Helps you access your true warrior nature.
Superb protection stone.
Supports you in overcoming your fears.
Represents strength and integrity.
A good meditation stone.
A great aid in dealing with fear of acknowledging your personal power.
Stimulates feelings of confidence and courage.
Outstanding energy shield.
A good balance tool for either too little or too much Yang energy.
Helps you deal with depression and the thoughts creating a wall of
        depression you just can't quite jump over.
Aids in working with lessons concerning physical death or
        life-threatening illnesses.
A good reminder that your only real battle is with your own nature
        and that you will ultimately conquer.
Reminds you that you can never be defeated as long as you are
        always true to your Self.

WINDOW CRYSTAL

A true Window Crystal is one that has a diamond shape in the center front of its faces (facets). The diamond shape often actually becomes a seventh face of the crystal (giving you a 7-Faceted Crystal in addition to a Window; see Transmitter Crystal). True Window faces are larger than other diamond-shaped formations you will find on crystals, large enough for you to easily look into and through the window into the crystal's interior.

The diamond in the Window Crystal creates an octahedron, symbolizing the meeting of the Upper and Lower Worlds or Planes of Existence, Spirit connecting with Matter. Your Window Crystal can remind you to maintain the conscious awareness of this connection.

Windows can be used in meditation for windows into your own nature or essence, or any other window you would like to look into or out of. What you see through your Window Crystal may not be what someone else would see at all. Windows are only openings that let you look through walls and other barriers. If you see a view you don't like through your Window, maybe all that is needed is for you to change your perspective or clean your inner window, your preconceived ideas about what you are seeing.

Use your Window Crystal as a tool to help you change your view and to check your progress as you move along. And watch how your view through your Window changes according to your moods, energy, experiences, and growth.

As a symbol in their own right, windows represent your ability to see through the illusion of the "wall" in front of you. While windows do not themselves generate light, they allow light to freely enter. And windows give you the ability to see in two directions at once. Windows also symbolize your openness, your willingness to let in new views, new horizons.

## WINDOW CRYSTAL QUICK REFERENCE:

Symbolizes the meeting of the Upper and Lower Planes of Existence.
Symbolizes your willingness to see through the barriers in front of you.
Represents your ability to see in two directions at once.
Represents your capacity to see through illusions, to experience new vistas.
Reminds you to be open to new points of view.
Clears your perception.
A good Dream Stone.
An excellent meditation tool.
Helps access past and parallel life experiences.
Allows access to parallel realities.
Helps you to more clearly see your present view of personal reality.
Excellent channelling tool.
Reminds you to focus your point of view, to get a clearer picture.
Excellent telepathic communication tool.
Outstanding divination tool.
Lets you access and "see" into probable realities.
A good mirror for checking your viewpoints, your opinions, your beliefs.
Reminds you to let in the Light.

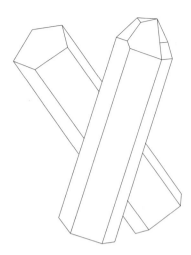

X CRYSTAL

An X Crystal is two crystals that have naturally grown together to form the letter X. This Crystal has a special ability to bring the Yin-Yang (female-male) energies into harmony and is often used in crystal layout patterns for this purpose, although X's are just slightly more Yang than Yin.

This is an excellent choice for someone in need of enhancing or getting in touch with their natural Yang characteristics, whether they are male or female. X Crystals are great energy rechargers and help you build and hold onto self-confidence and self-esteem. These are great supporters when you are reaching for well-balanced decisions, when your intent is to create win-win situations.

As a symbol, X Crystals represent the inversion of a thing, perfect balance and completion of a cycle through perfect balance, the Cross of St. Andrew, and the number 10. X also marks the spot, of course, and makes a great support during affirmations. This is the perfect partner for a Y Crystal

X CRYSTAL QUICK REFERENCE:

Symbolizes completion through perfect balance.
Symbolizes the inversion of a thing, stability, and the number 10.
Excellent protection stone.
Stimulates feelings of courage and self-confidence.
Good choice for programming or crystal layouts of any kind.
Helps balance Yin-Yang energies, with a slight emphasis on Yang.
Good choice for your natural masculine spiritual warrior nature.

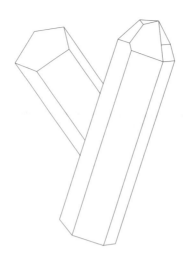

Y CRYSTAL

A Y Crystal is two quartz crystals that have grown together naturally to form the letter Y. A Y Crystal is a perfect companion for an X Crystal. Y Crystals have a special ability to help bring Yin-Yang (female-male) energies into balance and are often used in crystal layouts for this purpose, although they are just slightly more Yin in their energy.

This is a good choice for anyone in need of enhancing or getting in touch with their natural feminine spiritual characteristics, whether they are male or female. Y Crystals are good telepathic communication tools and help you get in touch with and learn not to fear your natural intuitive talents.

As a symbol, Y represents the gateway or the point of interpenetration. Pythagoras considered it the emblem for all human life, the foot or base symbolizing the innocence of the infant, and the dividing arms our adult choices between good and evil. Y also symbolizes the right and left hand paths, the dividing ways and crossroads presided over by various deities throughout human history.

Y CRYSTAL QUICK REFERENCE:

Symbolizes the gateway or point of interpenetration.
Represents humanity with its roots in innocence.
A good tool for developing your natural intuition and telepathic skills.
Superb choice for programming or crystal layouts of any kind.
Balances the Yin-Yang energies, with a slight emphasis on the Yin (feminine).
Good choice for reaching your female spiritual warrior nature.

# BIBLIOGRAPHY

Each book listed in this Bibliography is highly recommended to anyone interested in crystals, minerals, and the use of symbols in day-to-day living. Without the previous work of each of these authors this reference book would not have been possible.

*Colors and Crystals: A Journey Through the Chakras*, Joy Gardner, The Crossing Press, 1988.
*Crystal Enlightenment, Vol. I*, Katrina Raphael, Aurora Press, 1985.
*Crystal Healing: The Therapeutic Applications of Crystals and Stones, Vol 2*, Katrina Raphael, Aurora Press, 1987.
*The Crystalline Transmission: A Synthesis of Light, Vol. 3*, Katrina Raphael, Aurora Press, 1990.
*Crystal Wisdom, Spiritual Properties of Crystals & Gemstones*, Dolfyn, Earthspirit, Inc., 1989.
*A Dictionary of Symbols*, J.E. Cirlot, Dorset Press, 1991.
*Goddess In Every Woman: A New Psychology of Women*, Jean Shinoda Bolen, M.D., Harper Perennial, 1985.
*A Guide in Color to Precious and Semiprecious Stones*, Jaroslav Bauer and Vladimir Bousk, Chartwell Books, 1989.
*Lightseeds*, Wabun Wind & Alexander Reed, Prentice Hall, 1988.
*An Illustrated Encyclopedia of Traditional Symbols*, J.C. Cooper, Thames and Hudson, Ltd., 1992.
*Windows of Light: Quartz Crystals and Self-Transformation,* Randall N. & Vicki Baer, Harper & Row, 1984.
*Windows To The Mind: A Dream Symbol Guidebook*, Patricia Troyer, Stone People Publishing Company, 1995.
*The Woman's Encyclopedia of Myths and Secrets*, Barbara G. Walker, Harper Collins, 1983.

# ADDITIONAL READING

*The Complete Crystal Guidebook*, Uma Silby, Bantam Books, 1986.
*The Cosmic Crystal Spiral*, Ra Bonewitz, Element Books, 1986.
*Crystal Awareness*, Catherine Bowman, Llewellyn Publications, 1988.
*The Crystal Connection: A Guidebook for Personal & Planetary Ascension*, Randall N. & Vicki Baer, Harper & Row, 1987.
*The Crystal Handbook*, Kevin Sullivan, Signet Books, 1987.
*Crystal Healing: The Next Step*, Phyllis Galde, Llewellyn Publications, 1988.
*Love Is In The Earth: Laying-On-Of-Stones*, Melody, Earth-Love Publishing House, 1992.
*The Crystal Sourcebook: From Science to Metaphysics*, John Vincent Miewski, Virginia L. Harford, Mystical Publications, 1988.
*Gem Elixirs and Vibrational Healing, Vol. I & II,* Gurudas, Cassandra Press, 1985/86.
*Precious Stones, Their Healing Power and Planetary Influences*, Magda Palmer, St. Martin's Press, 1988.
*Rock Crystal: The Magic Stone*, Korra Deaver, Ph.D., Samuel Weiss, Inc., 1992.
*Stone Power*, Dorothee L. Mella, Warner Books, 1986.

# ORDER FORM

To order copies of *Crystal Personalities*, send requests along with payment to:

Stone People Publishing Company
7445 W. Cactus Rd., #211, Box 195
Peoria, AZ 85381

FOR PHONE ORDERS: 602-486-5149
FAX ORDERS: 602-486-0799

Book Price: $17.95 each US Dollars.
[Please call or write for multiple order discount prices].

SALES TAX:     Add 7.0% sales tax for books shipped in Arizona.

SHIPPING AND HANDLING COSTS: Book Rate $3.00 for the first book and 75 cents for each additional book. For UPS or air mail add $4.00 to total shipping.

SHIP TO:        _____

_____

_____

_____

NUMBER OF BOOKS ORDERED: _____

TOTAL AMOUNT DUE (including Sales Tax and Shipping Costs):
$    _____

PLEASE MAKE CHECK PAYABLE TO:
**Stone People Publishing Company**
[DO NOT SEND CASH]

Don't forget to ask about the *Crystal Personalities* 11∞15 Poster and our upcoming release, *Windows To The Mind: A Dream Symbol Guidebook.* Stone People also has soon-to-be-released information on other minerals. Write for details or to receive our free catalog.

Thank you for your order.

Stone People Publishing Company